Quarto.com

© 2023 Quarto Publishing Group USA Inc.
Text and photography © 2023 Jennifer Ziemons

First Published in 2023 by The Harvard Common Press,
an imprint of The Quarto Group,
100 Cummings Center, Suite 265-D,
Beverly, MA 01915, USA.
T (978) 282-9590   F (978) 283-2742

The Harvard Common Press titles are also available at discount for retail, wholesale, promotional, and bulk purchase. For details, contact the Special Sales Manager by email at specialsales@quarto.com or by mail at The Quarto Group, Attn: Special Sales Manager, 100 Cummings Center, Suite 265-D, Beverly, MA 01915, USA.

26 25 24 23   1 2 3 4 5

ISBN: 978-0-7603-8323-0

Digital edition published in 2023
eISBN: 978-0-7603-8324-7

Library of Congress Cataloging-in-Publication Data

Names: Ziemons, Jennifer, author.
Title: Tiny bakes : delicious mini cakes, pies, cookies, brownies, and more / Jennifer Ziemons.
Identifiers: LCCN 2023014533 (print) | LCCN 2023014534 (ebook) | ISBN 9780760383230 (hardcover) | ISBN 9780760383247 (ebook)
Subjects: LCSH: Baking. | Desserts. | LCGFT: Cookbooks.
Classification: LCC TX765 .Z44 2023 (print) | LCC TX765 (ebook) | DDC 641.81/5—dc23/eng/20230414

Design and page layout: Laura Shaw Design
Photography: Janos Vass
Illustration: Shutterstock

Printed in China

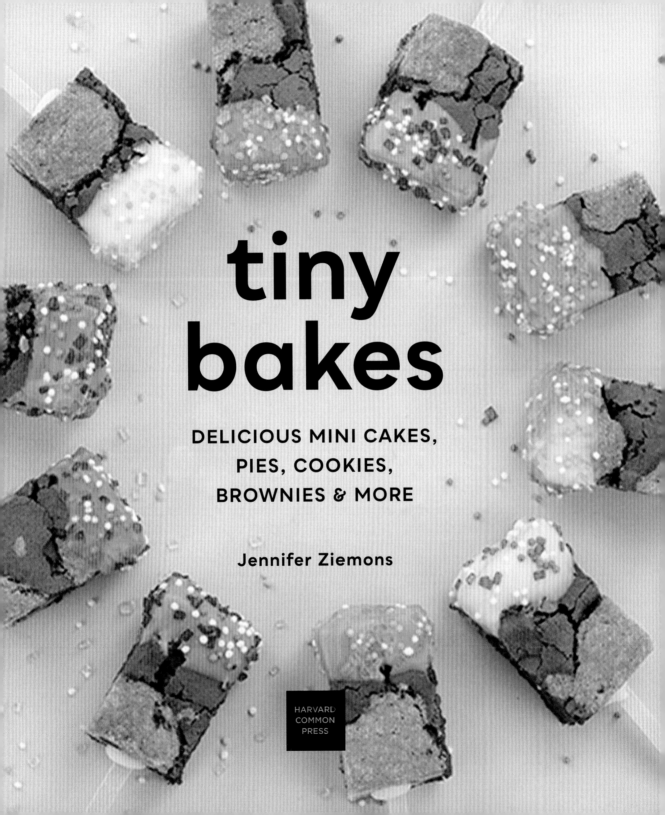

tiny
bakes

DELICIOUS MINI CAKES, PIES, COOKIES, BROWNIES & MORE

Jennifer Ziemons

HARVARD
COMMON
PRESS

Contents

1

Welcome to Tiny Baking

I am Jenny of Jenny's Mini Cooking Show, and I'll be your guide on this journey to becoming a mini master baker! You may already be experienced in the kitchen, in which case you'll just need a few tips and tricks for baking small. But if you are coming to the world of tiny baking with almost no experience, don't worry! In this book, I'll explain every step in detail so that you can succeed and amaze your family and friends with your tiny pastry creations.

For each recipe, I'll list the tools and ingredients you'll need and explain all the techniques you'll use to make a particular treat. For the decorations, follow my instructions at the beginning and then, once you've got the hang of it, let your imagination run wild and decorate the cakes, pies, brownies however *you* want! There are no limits!

Tiny-Baking Essentials

I know you want to get started, but first let me show you how baking mini treats is different from baking the desserts you normally bake. (You might be surprised, but there's not *too much* of a difference.)

First, the treats are much smaller. This means that making just one treat won't be enough! All the recipes in this book make multiple baked goods. You might also notice that the batch sizes in this book are odd from time to time. For example, why am I making ten cupcakes when a cupcake pan has space for twelve? Or why make five of something instead of a half dozen? Well, I first had to find the minimum amount that can be made with "normal" tools (e.g., the smallest amount of butter that can be beaten with a mixer).

Then, there are some ingredients, like eggs, that are hard to divide into small amounts. I often start with the ingredient that's the hardest to parcel out small and then base the measurements for all the other ingredients around it.

No matter, just like regular-size baking, these recipes are easy to scale up. If you want more, just double or triple the recipe! On the other hand, I do not recommend making half-recipes, as it can be hard to adequately mix very small amounts.

Since you'll be baking small treats, the baking time is often much shorter than in the case of their "big" counterparts. You will have to be very careful about this, as the treats can burn easily. Follow the instructions, and if you find your oven runs a little hotter than mine, cut back on the cooking time for the next batch.

If you don't want to buy a ton of specialty tools, here's the good news: You can prepare everything in this book with the "big" tools in your kitchen and just a few inexpensive special tools or pans. (That said, small tools can make mini baking more fun!)

THE TINY-BAKING TOOL KIT

Here's what you'll want to have on hand for the recipes in this book. Again, you don't need all these tools for every recipe—check the Tools and Materials section of each recipe for a precise list.

Mini cake pans: For mini baking, I recommend using cookie cutters as your cake pans. The recipes include the particular sizes and the amount of pans you would need to bake the entire recipe at once. But you can always bake in batches too. Here are the pans I recommend you have on hand, if you want to make everything in this book:

- About 2½ inches (6 cm) in diameter (six pieces)
- About 1½ inches (4 cm) in diameter (two pieces)
- About ¾ inch (2 cm) in diameter (two pieces)
- About ½ inch (1.25 cm) in diameter (one piece)
- About ¼ inch (0.6 cm) in diameter (one piece)

Mini cupcake pan: This is relatively inexpensive to purchase online. Look for one that makes 1¼- to 1½-inch (3- to 4-cm)-wide cupcakes.

Small pie pan: The pies in this book are all made with miniature 2½-inch (6-cm) pans. If you prefer to size up or size down a little, you'll need to adjust the recipes accordingly.

Small rolling pin: A 6-inch (15-cm) rolling pin makes life a little easier for some of the recipes in this book, though you can get away with a full-size one.

Baking sheet and cutting board: A regular size baking sheet and cutting board will work fine for these recipes, but the baking sheet in the photographs in this book is 4 x 9 inches (10 x 23 cm), and the cutting board is approximately 7 x 4 inches (18 x 10 cm).

Decorating nozzles: I use the smallest nozzles, ¼-inch (0.6-cm) size, for decorating. I use both the star-pattern and the round decorating nozzles.

Hand electric mixer: While all the recipes in the book have been scaled to work with a "normal"-size hand electric mixer, if you can find a smaller one (or small beaters for your mixer), your life will be even easier when you try to whip small amounts of butter! If you ever have trouble getting a good mix with your equipment, try doubling a batch size so that you have more to work with.

Optional baking supplies: In the photos I am using miniature items—they take the fun to another level! All are available online. The most popular are a kitchen spoon, approximately 5 to 6 inches (13 to 15 cm); a silicone spoon, approximately 5 to 6 inches (13 to 15 cm); a 4-inch (10-cm) metal bowl; a 4-inch (10-cm) metal pot; and a 5-inch (13-cm) cake stand.

Other essentials: You should also have a sieve and food coloring (and sometimes a food coloring pen too) handy.

A Tiny-Baking Quick Start Guide

1. Put on an apron to protect your clothes. (Tiny baking can still be messy from time to time!)

2. Always clean the work surface you'll be working on. This is very important! Then wipe it completely dry. Wash your hands with soap as well (you will have to do this several times during the baking process).

3. Before beginning to bake, read the whole recipe and study the photos. It's important to keep your surroundings tidy and clean while baking, too, and to pack away what you will no longer use.

4. Okay, get your tools. If you are using something for the first time or you think it is not clean enough, wash it! Then dry it and put it on a clean work surface. Once you have all your tools ready, grab the ingredients listed for the recipe. You can also measure them out in advance. (Always sift the dry ingredients so that they don't remain lumpy. And use an accurate kitchen scale!)

5. When removing the baking pans or sheets from the oven, always use oven mitts or heat-proof gloves specifically designed for this purpose!

Patience is very important! Small cakes are often more difficult to prepare than large ones. Don't rush, and don't be afraid to try a recipe again if it didn't turn out perfect the first time.

Let your imagination run wild. Imagine that you shrunk and that's why you make mini cakes and "need" smaller-size utensils to really embrace it!

Now that we've covered all the important stuff, let's dive in. Are you ready to enter this magical, fun world? Grab your apron and get started!

TIPS FOR SUCCESS

- **General safety:** Never leave empty cookware on the stove or food unattended on the stove or in an oven. Never touch hot cookware or baking pans without proper protective gloves! Keep the stove clean so that there is nothing on it that could start a fire.

- **Getting ready and cleaning up:** Remove any rings or bracelets that could get caught in the tools. Switch off all electronic devices after use: oven, stove, hand mixer, etc. Before turning the oven on, check that there is nothing inside it. Always set it to the required temperature and double-check that it has preheated before baking.

- **Stand and hand mixers:** Be careful with the electric hand mixer! As it runs on electricity, some parts of the mixer cannot be exposed to liquid. Plus, you can easily get your fingers caught in the paddles.

- **Bake times:** Tiny items tend to bake much faster than big ones, so you have to be very careful when baking. If the top of somehing gets brown quickly, lower the heat. Keep your eye on everything the first time you bake it.

- **Fruit and mix-in sizes:** Cut any fruit or large toppings/mix-in items at least five times smaller than for the big cakes.

- **Pie crusts:** Make sure that you roll crusts out much thinner than for large pies (aim for at least a third as thin).

- **Food coloring:** Since you're making tiny cakes, you need much less food coloring. Sometimes just one or two drops is enough.

2

Cupcakes & Cake Pops

Monster Cupcakes

Anyone who loves monsters will fall in love with these adorable cupcakes. And who doesn't love monsters when they are sweet and colorful? Copy the colors here or get creative with your own color choices. Then make the cupcakes even more unique with different mouths or eyes. They are perfect for Halloween parties, but are also great for birthday parties or end-of-the-school-year celebrations.

Tools & Materials

Small cupcake pan

Small cupcake liners (about ½ inch [1.25 cm] in diameter)

Piping bags

Electric mixer

Toothpicks

Grass-pattern decorating nozzle (about ½ inch [1.25 cm] in diameter)

YIELD: 12 CUPCAKES

IMPORTANT This design requires toothpicks to stay together. Be very careful when eating and always place a note on the plate when sharing!

FOR CUPCAKES

60 g all-purpose flour
60 g granulated sugar
½ teaspoon baking powder
Pinch of salt
10 g unsalted butter, softened
2 teaspoons honey
33 g whole milk
50 g eggs (1 large egg)
Food coloring: pink, purple, blue, green

FOR FROSTING

45 g white chocolate
60 g unsalted butter, softened
75 g powdered sugar
½ teaspoon vanilla extract
31 g heavy cream
Food coloring: pink, purple, blue, green

FOR DECORATION

50 g white fondant icing paste
10 g black fondant icing paste
Food coloring: pink, purple, blue, green

TO MAKE THE CUPCAKES

1. Preheat the oven to 400°F (205°C, or gas mark 6). Line a small cupcake pan with paper or silicone cupcake liners.

2. In a small bowl, whisk the flour, sugar, baking powder, and salt.

3. In a small microwave-safe bowl or measuring cup, combine the butter, honey, and milk. Heat for 45 seconds on high, or until the butter starts melting. Remove from the microwave and stir to melt the butter completely. Mix the egg with these wet ingredients.

4. Add the wet ingredients to the dry ingredients and stir to combine.

5. Divide the batter into 4 small bowls. Add pink, purple, blue, and green food coloring to each bowl to achieve the desired shades.

6. Fill a piping bag with the batter and cut the tip of the bag. Fill the paper-lined cupcake pans with the batter. Do not fill the pans fully—leave an inch or so empty at the top; otherwise, the cupcakes will spill out of the pan during baking. Bake until a toothpick inserted in the center comes out clean, about 15 minutes. Cool for 5 minutes before transferring the cupcakes from the pan to a wire rack. Cool completely before decorating. **A**

A

TO MAKE THE FROSTING

1. Place the white chocolate in a small heat-proof bowl and microwave for 30 seconds. Stir well, then put back in the microwave and heat in 15-second units—stirring well in between—until the chocolate is completely smooth.

2. Set the chocolate aside to cool for at least 15 minutes, until it is no longer warm to the touch (otherwise it will melt the butter in the next step).

3. While the chocolate is cooling, beat the butter at medium speed in a small bowl until creamy, using an electric mixer. Gradually add the powdered sugar and scrape the sides and bottom of the bowl periodically to ensure that all the ingredients are well combined.

B

4. Once the white chocolate has cooled to room temperature, pour it into the butter mixture and beat on a low speed until fully combined.

5. Add the vanilla extract and stir well.

6. With the electric mixer on low speed, gradually add the heavy cream. Slowly increase the speed to high and beat for 30 to 60 seconds or until the desired consistency is reached.

7. Divide this cream into 4 small bowls and color the frosting in each bowl (just as you did with the batter).

C

D

E

F

TO ASSEMBLE THE CUPCAKES

1. While you wait for the cupcakes to cool, make the monsters' mouths and eyes.

2. Divide the white fondant paste into 5 parts. Leave 1 part white and color the remaining 4 the same way you did with the batter and the frosting (pink, purple, blue, and green).

3. Make 6 balls smaller than ½ inch [1.25 cm] in diameter of each of the 4 colors. Stick them on toothpicks.

4. Knead the black fondant a little by hand to soften it, then roll it really thin with the rolling pin. Cut out 12 semicircles, about ½ inch (1.25 cm) in diameter, and pull the corners up a little to form mouth shapes. Roll out the white fondant and cut out little teeth. Place 3 teeth on every mouth shape: 2 on the top and 1 on the bottom. With the remaining white fondant, cut out circles of about ¼ inch (0.6 cm) in diameter. Using a little water, stick them on the colorful balls on the toothpicks. This will be the white part of the eye. Place a small black glob on top of each white eye for the pupil. **B**

5. Put one of the frostings (for example, purple) in a piping bag fitted with the grass-pattern decorating nozzle. Take the 3 purple-color cupcake bottoms. Put a tiny dot of frosting in the middle of the side of the cupcake facing you and stick a mouth on it, then pipe the tiny imitation "hair" on the whole cupcake. Repeat with the remaining 3 colors of cupcakes and frosting. **C, D, E**

6. Once you're done, stick the toothpicks with the eyes on them in the middle of the cupcakes. **F**

Important! Be careful not to mix the colors. For example, use the pink frosting and pink eyes with the pink cupcakes.

Bonfire Cupcakes

Get in the camping spirit with these cupcakes—complete with tiny marshmallows. You're definitely not going to get burned, even though it looks like a real fire is crackling away on top of the crispy pretzels! Don't limit these adorable cakes to outdoor adventures. Spice up a barbecue with them. Or pair them with the Bee or Frog Cake Pops (pages 39 and 31) for an outdoor-themed party.

FOR CUPCAKES
30 g eggs (about ⅔ large egg)
33 g unsalted butter, softened
½ teaspoon vanilla extract
66 g all-purpose flour
¼ teaspoon baking powder
¼ teaspoon baking soda
5 g cocoa powder
50 g granulated sugar
60 g orange juice

FOR FROSTING
30 g unsalted butter, softened
80 g powdered sugar
7.5 g heavy cream
½ teaspoon vanilla extract
Juice from half an orange
Food coloring: yellow, orange, red

FOR DECORATION
10 to 15 pretzels
20 small marshmallows

Tools & Materials
Small cupcake pan
Small cupcake liners (about ½ inch [1.25 cm] in diameter)
Electric mixer
Plastic wrap
Piping bags
Star-pattern decorating nozzle (about ¼ inch [0.6 cm] in diameter)
Toothpicks

YIELD: 10 CUPCAKES

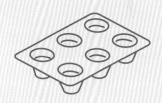

TO MAKE THE CUPCAKES

1. Preheat the oven to 375°F (190°C, or gas mark 5). Line a small cupcake pan with paper or silicone cupcake liners.

2. In a small bowl, beat the egg well, then add the butter and vanilla extract and combine them.

3. In another small bowl, sift the flour, baking powder, baking soda, and cocoa powder together. Add the sugar and mix.

4. To the butter mixture, add the dry ingredients in two additions and then the orange juice. Mix thoroughly using an electric mixer.

5. Scoop the batter into the cupcake liners. Do not fill the pans fully—leave an inch or so empty at the top—otherwise, the cupcakes will spill out of the pan during baking. **A**

A

6. Bake for 20 to 25 minutes. They are ready when the top of the cupcakes spring back on touch.

7. Let cool on a wire rack before decorating.

TO MAKE THE FROSTING

1. With an electric mixer, beat the butter on medium speed until creamy, about 1 minute. Add the powdered sugar, heavy cream, and vanilla extract. Beat on low speed for 30 seconds, then increase to medium-high speed and beat for 1 minute. Taste, then add the orange juice.

2. Divide the frosting into 3 parts by pouring into 3 small bowls. Color each frosting with yellow, orange, and red food coloring until you get the desired colors.

TO ASSEMBLE THE CUPCAKES

1. Slice a thin layer off the tops of the cupcakes to create a flat surface. **B**

2. Break or cut the pretzels into 1-inch (2.5-cm) pieces. Put a small dot of frosting in the middle of each cupcake and lay the pretzels on top of it like logs for a campfire. **C**

3. Put the 3 kinds of frosting into 3 separate piping bags with a star-pattern nozzle. Lay an 8 x 8-inch (20 x 20-cm) square-shaped plastic wrap on the table. Draw strips of the 3 types of frostings one after the other on the plastic wrap. Once all the frosting is spread, grab the 2 ends of the plastic wrap and roll it up. Cut off 1 end and place it in a new piping bag with a star-pattern nozzle. This will give the frosting a striped pattern when you squeeze it out. **D, E, F**

4. Pipe a swirl of frosting onto the cupcake imitating a fire. **G**

5. Stick a marshmallow on a toothpick. You can roast it a bit with a matchstick if you'd like. Insert it into the cupcake, near the "fire" frosting. **H**

B

C

D

E

F

G

H

Unicorn Cupcakes

A cupcake with all the colors of a rainbow. When you bite into one, it's not only delicious but also hides a little surprise! You can fill the inside with anything fun: think sprinkles, chocolate, gummy candies, or jam. Let your friends know about the rainbow filling, or tell them to take a bite and find the surprise on their own.

FOR CUPCAKES

30 g unsalted butter, softened
57 g granulated sugar
30 g eggs (about ⅔ large egg)
124 g whole milk
¼ teaspoon almond extract
75 g all-purpose flour
½ teaspoon baking powder
Pinch of salt
110 g chopped fresh strawberries

FOR FROSTING

100 g marzipan paste
114 g whole milk
¼ packet vanilla pudding
¼ teaspoon sugar
31 g unsalted butter, softened
Food coloring: blue, green, purple, yellow, pink

FOR DECORATION

50 g white fondant icing paste
Food coloring: yellow, pink

Tools & Materials

Electric mixer

Small cupcake pan

Small cupcake liners (about ½ inch [1.25 cm] in diameter)

Piping bags

Plastic wrap

Star-pattern decorating nozzle (about ¼ inch [0.6 cm] in diameter)

YIELD: 10 CUPCAKES

TIP When making the frosting, always make sure that all the ingredients are at the same temperature; otherwise, the butter will condense.

TO MAKE THE CUPCAKES

1. Preheat the oven to 375°F (190°C, or gas mark 5). Line a small cupcake pan with paper or silicone cupcake liners.

2. In a medium-size bowl, cream together the butter and sugar.

3. Add the egg gradually, beating well after each addition.

4. Add the milk and almond extract and beat until combined.

5. In a small bowl, whisk together flour, baking powder, and salt. Add dry ingredients to the butter mixture and stir to combine (do not beat or overmix).

6. Cut the strawberries into very tiny pieces. Mix them into the batter. **A**

7. Scoop the batter into the cupcake liners. Do not fill the cupcake liners fully—leave an inch or so empty at the top—otherwise, the cupcakes will spill out of the liners during baking. **B**

8. Bake for 20 to 25 minutes until golden brown.

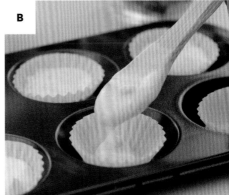

TO MAKE THE FROSTING

1. Cut the marzipan paste into very small pieces. **C**

2. Bring the milk to a boil in a small saucepan, then remove from the heat and stir in the sugar and vanilla pudding. Stir until lump-free. Then add half of the marzipan pieces and stir over the heat until you get a creamy consistency.

3. Remove from the heat and let cool.

4. Beat the butter with a hand electric mixer until fluffy.

5. Gradually add the pudding mixture, a little at a time, until completely blended.

6. Then add the remaining marzipan and mix until you have a nice, smooth frosting.

7. Divide the frosting into 5 small bowls. Color each frosting with food coloring to create a pale shade (blue, green, purple, yellow, pink).

TO ASSEMBLE THE CUPCAKES

1. Use a small spoon or knife to carve a small hole in the middle of each cupcake to hide the sprinkles (or whatever filling you like). **D**

2. Put the 5 kinds of frosting into 5 separate piping bags. Lay an 8 x 8-inch (20 x 20-cm) square-shaped plastic wrap on the table. Draw strips of the 5 types of frosting one after the other on the plastic wrap. Once all the frosting is spread, grab the 2 ends of the plastic wrap and roll it up. Cut off 1 end and place that frosting in a new piping bag with the star-pattern nozzle. This will give the frosting a striped pattern when you squeeze out. **E**

3. Press a nice swirl of frosting on top of each cupcake. **F**

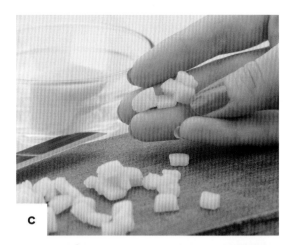

C

D

E

F

G

H

4. You can leave the cupcakes just as they are or decorate them with the sprinkles you hid inside (if you chose to do so). Or you can even make a unicorn cupcake. You will need a horn and 2 ears to do this.

5. Take about 5 g of the fondant icing paste and color it with a little yellow food coloring. This will make the horns. Color another 5 g pink and leave the rest white.

MAKE THE HORN

1. To do this, roll out 2 very thin 2-inch (5-cm)-long cylindrical shapes of the yellow fondant. Lay them side by side, pinch the 2 together at the top, then roll them on top of each other. You will need a horn about 1 inch (2.5 cm) long, so cut the fondant there. **G**

2. For the ears, roll out the white fondant real thin. Cut out circles of about 1 inch (2.5 cm) in diameter using a cookie cutter. Cut them in half and shape ears from it. Do the same with the pink fondant, but this time cut out ½-inch (1.25-cm) circles, cut in half, and shape. Once they're done, stick the pink ears onto the white ones. Now the ears are ready.

3. Take a cupcake. Press the unicorn horn just in the middle and the 2 ears on the sides. **H**

And there you go!
Your magical cupcakes
are ready!

Ice Cream Cone Cake Pops

I scream, you scream, we all scream for these adorable ice cream cone cake pops! Sometimes I'm in the mood to spend hours making something with tons of detail, but other times, I just love easy cake pops like these. There's even no need for rolling perfectly shaped spheres. So be creative, be imperfect, but most of all, have some fun while making these.

Tools & Materials

Electric mixer

Small saucepan and heat-proof metal bowl (see Tip on page 40)

Piping bag

YIELD: 20 CAKE POPS, SMALLER THAN ½ INCH (1.25 CM) EACH

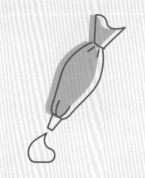

FOR CAKE POPS

21 g cream cheese, softened

17 g granulated sugar

10 fresh raspberries, washed and dried

12 g whipped cream

50 g graham crackers

30 mini ice cream cones (If you cannot find mini cones, you can cut off the end of regular cones.)

FOR DECORATION

50 g white chocolate callets

Food coloring: blue (or whatever color you choose)

10 g milk chocolate

Sprinkles

TO MAKE THE CAKE POPS

1. Place the cream cheese and the sugar in a bowl and whip with a hand electric mixer. Add in the raspberries and stir to combine. Make sure to break up the raspberries and incorporate into the cream cheese. Add in the whipped cream and stir with a spoon or spatula (not an electric mixer).

2. Put the graham crackers in a sealable bag and crush them into small pieces using a rolling pin. If you have a food chopper at hand, you can use that. Add the crumbs to the raspberry cream.

3. Fill the mini cones with the mixture until full, then shape balls of about ½ inch (1.25 cm) in diameter from the remaining mixture. Put the cones and the balls in the freezer to set, about 10 minutes. **A**

A

E

F

4. After the mini ice cream cones have chilled, top each one with a little melted chocolate, then attached a frozen cake pop ball on top. Put these back in the fridge. **B**

5. Melt a small amount of the white chocolate callets over boiling water, stirring constantly. Stir with a metal spoon until the chocolate is melted, then remove from the heat. Color the melted chocolate with blue food coloring (or any other color you like) to achieve the desired shade.

6. Take the cake pops out of the freezer. Holding by the cone, dip the ball in the melted white chocolate. If necessary, use a spoon to completely coat the ball with chocolate, then remove the ball from the bowl, letting the excess chocolate drip into the bowl. **C, D**

7. Refrigerate for 10 minutes to let the chocolate set.

8. Now melt the milk chocolate. Once melted, place in a piping bag and drizzle the top of each cake pop. Before the chocolate sets, add the colored sprinkles. Put the pops back in the fridge until they're ready to serve. **E, F**

Aren't they adorable?
And they are absolutely delicious!

Frog Cake Pops

Some people love frogs, and some people think of them as "icky," just like snakes and lizards! Well, I think even if you are in that latter camp, there's no denying these tiny frog cake pops are charming! They will rock any festive occasion and are especially fun for water celebrations—like a pool party. Draw them with any face you want: smiling, grumpy, laughing, crying—it's up to you. Cut out some simple "lily pads" out of green napkins and you're all set to serve!

Tools & Materials

Small baking pan (about 4 inches [10 cm] in diameter)

Parchment paper

Electric mixer

Small saucepan and heat-proof metal bowl (see Tip on page 40)

Toothpicks

Rolling pin

Super-tiny round cookie cutter

YIELD: 30 CAKE POPS, SMALLER THAN ½ INCH (1.25 CM) EACH

FOR CAKE POPS

52 g all-purpose flour
¼ teaspoon baking powder
Pinch of baking soda
Pinch of salt
29 g unsalted butter, softened
50 g granulated sugar
15 g eggs (about ⅓ large egg)
½ teaspoon vanilla extract
60 g whole milk
15 g peach jam
15 g melted unsalted butter

FOR DECORATION

50 g white chocolate callets
Food coloring: green
10 g white fondant icing paste
Black food coloring pen
Sprinkles

TO MAKE THE CAKE

1. Preheat the oven to 350°F (177°C, or gas mark 4). Grease and lightly flour a square baking pan or line it with parchment paper.

2. Whisk the flour, baking powder, baking soda, and salt in a small bowl. Set aside. Using an electric mixer, beat the butter and sugar in a small bowl until creamy, about 2 minutes. Add the egg and vanilla extract and beat on high speed until combined. Scrape down the bottom and sides of the bowl as needed.

3. With the mixer on low speed, add the dry ingredients and the milk to the wet ingredients until fully combined. Manually whisk the batter to ensure there are no large lumps at the bottom of the bowl. The batter will be slightly thick. Pour the batter evenly into the prepared pan. Do not fill the pans fully—leave an inch or so empty at the top—otherwise, the cake will spill out of the pan during baking.

A

B

C

4. Bake for 30 minutes or until a toothpick inserted in the center comes out clean.

5. Let the cake cool completely in the pan placed on a wire rack.

6. Remove the cooled cake from the baking pan and trim off the edges.

TO MAKE THE CAKE POPS

1. Crumble the cake into a medium-size bowl. Make sure there are no large chunks. **A**

2. Add the jam and butter, then combine. **B**

3. Form balls of about ½ inch (1.25 cm) in diameter by hand, then place them on a parchment paper–lined baking sheet. **C**

4. Take a small saucepan and a heat-proof metal bowl that matches in size. Bring the water in the saucepan to a boil.

5. Melt a small amount of the white chocolate callets in the heat-proof bowl over the saucepan of simmering water (don't let the bowl touch the water), stirring constantly with a metal spoon until the chocolate is melted, then remove from the heat. Color the melted chocolate with green food coloring to achieve the desired shade. Dip a toothpick into the green chocolate and then insert it into the cake ball. Repeat until all the balls are on sticks. Freeze the balls with the toothpicks in for at least a half hour. **D**

6. While the balls are freezing, make the eyes for the frogs. Knead the white fondant a little by hand to soften it, then roll it really thin with a rolling pin. Cut out the eyes with the tiny round cookie cutter. Once you've got all the pieces needed, draw the pupils on the eyes using a black food coloring pen. **E**

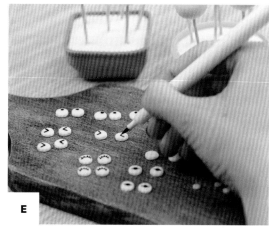

D · E

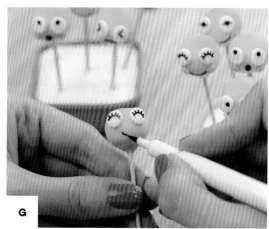

F · G

7. Take the cake balls out of the freezer. Holding by the toothpick, dip each ball in the melted chocolate. If necessary, use a spoon to completely coat the ball with chocolate, then remove the ball from the bowl, letting the excess chocolate drip into the bowl. **F**

8. Poke the cake pops into a piece of foam board. Refrigerate for 10 minutes.

9. Once the cake pops are chilled, you can start decorating them with the eyes. Place a tiny drop of chocolate on the back of an eye to stick to the cake pop. Repeat until all the frogs have 2 eyes. Next, draw a mouth to match the eyes. If you want, you can put rainbow sprinkles on the edges of the lips. **G**

Octopus Cake Pops

Imagine a plate full of tiny octopus cake pops in all colors of the rainbow. Draw happy smiles, surprised faces, or heart-shaped eyes for Valentine's Day treats. For other holidays, it's easy to give them a little remix: Decorate them with little rabbit ears or Santa hats. No matter when you're serving them, they are sure to bring smiles and mesmerize your guests with their tiny little tentacles!

FOR CAKE POPS

31 g unsalted butter, softened
31 g milk chocolate
45 g eggs (about 1 large egg)
84 g granulated sugar
29 g all-purpose flour
7.5 g cocoa powder
¼ teaspoon vanilla extract
Pinch of salt

FOR DECORATION

50 g colorful white chocolate callets (If you can't find blue ones, or the color you want, you can use food coloring to color white chocolate. Add as many drops as necessary until you get the desired color.)
Black food coloring pen

Tools & Materials

Small baking pan (about 4 inches [10 cm] in diameter)

Parchment paper

Small saucepan and heat-proof metal bowl (see Tip on page 40)

Electric mixer

Toothpicks

Piping bags

A piece of paper to draw the tentacles

YIELD: 30 CAKE POPS, SMALLER THAN ½ INCH (1.25 CM) EACH

TO MAKE THE CAKE

1. Preheat the oven to 350°F (177°C, or gas mark 4) or 320°F (160°C, or gas mark 3) fan forced. Grease and lightly flour a square baking pan or line it with parchment paper.

2. Take a small saucepan and a heat-proof metal bowl that matches in size. Bring the water in the saucepan to a boil.

3. Place the butter and chocolate in the heat-proof bowl over the saucepan of simmering water (don't let the bowl touch the water). Stir with a metal spoon until the chocolate is melted, then remove from the heat. **A**

4. With a hand electric mixer, quickly stir in the egg, sugar, flour, cocoa powder, vanilla extract, and salt until just combined. Pour the mixture into the prepared baking pan. Bake for 30 minutes or until a toothpick inserted in the center comes out with moist crumbs on it. Set aside to cool completely.

5. Remove the cooled cake from the baking pan and trim off the edges. You won't need the edges, so wrap them and put away. These will be good for a snack later!

A

B

TO MAKE THE CAKE POPS

1. Crumble the cake into a bowl. Form balls smaller than ½ inch (1.25 cm) in diameter by hand, then place them on a parchment paper–lined baking sheet.

2. Now it's time to use the saucepan and the metal bowl again (make sure they are cleaned well before you start with this!). Melt a small amount of the blue chocolate callets over the boiling water, stirring constantly. Insert a toothpick into the blue chocolate and then insert into the cake ball. Repeat until all the balls are on sticks. Freeze the balls with the toothpicks in for at least 2 hours.

3. While the balls are freezing, draw the legs of the octopus on a piece of paper, then place a piece of white parchment paper on top to make the pattern transparent. **B**

4. Place the blue melted chocolate into a piping bag (if you feel that the chocolate has solidified, remelt it). Cut a small hole at the tip of the bag. Start piping a tentacle first and outline the circle as you go into each tentacle. When ready, pour the remaining chocolate back into the bowl.

5. Take the cake balls out of the freezer. Holding by the toothpick, dip a ball in the melted chocolate. If necessary, use a spoon to completely coat the ball with chocolate, then remove the ball from the bowl, letting the excess chocolate drip into the bowl. Put it immediately on the parchment paper to dry. Try placing it on the tentacles right in the middle. This way the ball (the body of the octopus) will stick to the tentacles. Let these sit for about 10 to 15 minutes to ensure the chocolate has completely hardened. **C**

c

6. After they are hardened, prepare the eyes of the octopus. Melt some white chocolate and place 2 white dots on the body of the octopus using a piping bag. Think about where the eyes should be and draw them there. Using chocolate tinted with black food coloring, draw the black part of the eyes and the mouth. (You can also use a black food coloring pen.)

7. Carefully remove each octopus off the paper. Place them on a plate and serve!

Bee Cake Pops

Bzzz bzzz . . . what's that? They are small, cute, and flying from flower to flower. Fortunately, these bees are all sweet and no sting. These little cake pops are delicious fun for parties and spreads of all sorts. Decorate with artificial flowers or even bits of edible honeycomb (see Tip below, right) to take this themed treat over the top.

FOR CAKE POPS

50 g all-purpose flour
10 g cocoa powder
70 g granulated sugar
¼ teaspoon baking powder
Pinch of salt
20 g unsalted butter, softened
60 g whole milk
30 g eggs (about ⅔ large egg)
½ teaspoon vanilla extract
20 g pineapple juice
15 g melted unsalted butter

FOR DECORATION

50 g white chocolate callets
Tiny black sugar beads
Food coloring: yellow, black
Black food coloring pen

Tools & Materials

Small baking pan (about 4 inches [10 cm] in diameter)

Electric mixer

Small saucepan and heat-proof metal bowl (see Tip on page 40)

Toothpicks

A piece of paper to draw the wings of the bees and parchment paper

Piping bags

YIELD: 30 CAKE POPS, SMALLER THAN ½ INCH (1.25 CM) EACH

TIP Melt extra white chocolate and color it a yellowish-brown shade and spread it on bubble wrap to imitate honeycomb. Put this in the fridge so that it can set. Place the cake pops on top to serve. But remember, you cannot eat the bubble wrap!

TO MAKE THE CAKE

1. Preheat the oven to 350°F (177°C, or gas mark 4). Grease and lightly flour a square baking pan or line it with parchment paper.

2. Put the flour, cocoa powder, sugar, baking powder, salt, and butter in a stand mixer with a paddle attachment. You can also use a bowl and a hand electric mixer. Mix the ingredients until you get a sandy consistency.

3. Whisk the milk, egg, and vanilla extract in a cup, then slowly pour into the flour mixture and beat until smooth and well mixed. Scrape down the bottom and sides of the bowl as needed. The batter will be slightly thick.

4. Pour the batter evenly into the pan. Don't fill the pan fully—leave an inch or so empty at the top—otherwise, the cake will spill out of the pan during baking. Bake for 30 minutes or until a toothpick inserted in the center comes out clean.

A

5. Let the cake cool completely in the pan placed on a wire rack.

6. Remove the cooled cake from the baking pan and trim off the edges.

TO MAKE THE CAKE POPS

1. Crumble the trimmed cake into a medium-size bowl. Make sure there are no large chunks. **A**

2. Add the pineapple juice and butter, then combine the mixture.

3. Form slightly elongated balls of about ½ inch (1.25 cm) in diameter by hand, then place them on a parchment paper–lined baking sheet. **B**

4. Take a small saucepan and a heat-proof metal bowl that matches in size. Bring the water in the saucepan to a boil.

5. Melt a small amount of the white chocolate callets over the boiling water, stirring constantly with a metal spoon until they are melted, then remove from the heat. Set aside 30 g of this melted chocolate in a small bowl. This will make the wings. Then put another 10 g in a separate bowl and add black food coloring. You'll use that to draw the stripes on the bee's back. Color the remaining chocolate with yellow food coloring to achieve the desired shade.

B

6. Dip a toothpick into the yellow chocolate and insert into a cake ball. Repeat until all the balls are on sticks. Freeze the balls with the toothpicks in for at least a half hour. **C**

7. While the balls are freezing, make the wings for the bees. Draw the wings in semicircle shapes on a piece of white paper. Make it roughly ½ inch (1.25 cm) in diameter. Then place a piece of parchment paper on top of the white paper to make the pattern transparent. Take a piping bag and pour in the melted white chocolate that you have set aside. Cut a small hole at the end of the bag, then pipe the bee's wings onto the parchment paper, following the lines drawn on the paper. Refrigerate for a few minutes to allow the chocolate to solidify. **D**

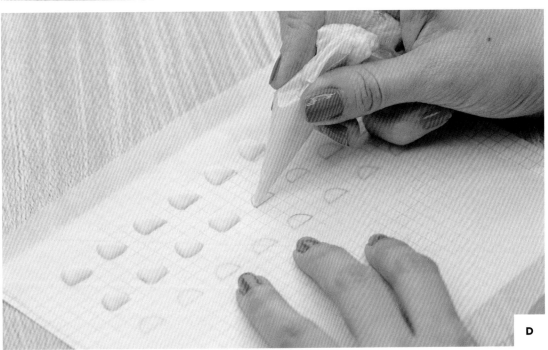

E

8. Take the cake balls out of the freezer. Holding by the toothpick, dip a ball in the melted yellow chocolate. If necessary, use a spoon to completely coat the ball with chocolate, then lift the ball up, letting the excess chocolate drip into the bowl. (Re-melt the yellow chocolate at any time if necessary.) **E**

9. Poke the cake pops into a piece of foam board by the toothpicks. Refrigerate for 10 minutes.

10. Once you have all the cake pops, you can start decorating. Pour the melted black chocolate into a piping bag. (If it has solidified in the meantime, melt it again.) Cut a small hole at the end of the piping bag. Hold a cake pop by the toothpick in 1 hand and draw 3 stripes on its back with your other hand. Once you've got the stripes on one bee, immediately attach its white wings so that they can stick to the black chocolate. **F**

F

11. The next step is making the eyes. Using a piping bag filled with white chocolate, pipe tiny eyes onto the bee and immediately press a tiny black sugar bead into their center. Now all you have to do is draw the tiny mouth with the black food coloring pen! **G**

Have you ever seen so many delightful bees? Serve them creatively!

G

Cakes

Three-Tier Celebration Cakes

Planning a wedding shower? Or do you just want to surprise someone with a mini tier cake? No matter, just know that when you ask if they love this cake, they will say "I do!" This design is also great for birthdays, Mother's Day, or any special (okay, even just special-ish) occasion.

FOR CAKES

20 cocktail cherries
85 g all-purpose flour
¼ teaspoon baking powder
Pinch of salt
45 g egg whites (2 egg whites)
36 g cherry juice
43 g whole milk
½ teaspoon vanilla extract
13 g vegetable oil
56 g unsalted butter, softened
100 g granulated sugar
23 g milk chocolate chips

FOR FROSTING

28 g unsalted butter, softened
150 g powdered sugar
¼ teaspoon heavy cream
¼ teaspoon vanilla extract

FOR DECORATION

5 g of each: pink, blue, and white fondant icing paste
Tiny sugar beads (pink, blue, and yellow)

Tools & Materials

Nine cake pans (3 pans for 1 cake: 2½ inches [6 cm], 1½ inches [4 cm], and 1 inch [2.5 cm] in diameter)

Parchment paper

Electric mixer

Piping bags

Round decorating nozzle (about ½ inch [1.25 cm] in diameter)

Cake stand (rotating optional)

Cake spatula

Rolling pin

Flower-shaped cookie cutters (about ¼ inch [0.6 cm] to about ½ inch [1.25 cm] in diameter, various sizes)

YIELD: 3 CAKES (3 CAKES, 3 TIERS EACH)

TO MAKE THE CAKES

1. Preheat the oven to 350°F (177°C, or gas mark 4). Grease and lightly flour the cake pans or line them with parchment paper.

2. Rinse the cocktail cherries in a fine mesh strainer and dry well with a paper towel, then chop them fine.

3. Sift the flour, baking powder, and salt together in a small bowl.

4. In another small bowl, put the egg whites, cherry juice, milk, vanilla extract, and vegetable oil. Combine with a fork.

5. In the small bowl of your electric mixer, beat the butter at medium speed. Add the sugar and continue beating until light in color and fluffy, about 3 minutes.

A

B

C

D

6. Add about half of the flour mixture into this bowl and mix on low speed until just blended. Add half of the wet ingredients too and blend. Continue alternating the dry and wet ingredients (the last turn should be dry ingredients) until combined. Do not overbeat this mixture.

7. Gently stir the chopped cherries and chocolate chips into the batter. **A**

8. Pour the batter into each of the 9 prepared cake pans, dividing evenly. Do not fill the pans fully. Leave an inch or so empty at the top—otherwise, the cakes will spill out of the pan during baking. **B**

9. Bake for 30 to 35 minutes. When the cakes spring back on touch or a toothpick inserted into the center comes out clean or with only a few crumbs attached, the cakes are done. Let the cakes cool in their pans for 10 minutes. Then, carefully remove the cakes from the cake pans and place on a wire rack to cool completely.

TO MAKE THE FROSTING

1. With an electric mixer on medium speed, beat the butter in a small bowl until fluffy. Add the powdered sugar gradually and beat until light and fluffy.

2. Add the heavy cream, a little at a time, until the frosting is stretchy in consistency. Mix in the vanilla extract until the frosting is smooth and creamy.

TO ASSEMBLE THE CAKES

1. After removing the cakes from the pans, slice a thin layer off the top of each cake to create a flat surface. Three cakes are needed for one cake: one of each size.

2. Fill a piping bag fitted with the round decorating nozzle of ½ inch (1.25 cm) with the frosting. Press a small dot of frosting in the middle of the cake stand and place the first, biggest (2½ inches [6 cm]) cake on it. Cover the top of the cake with a portion of the white frosting and smooth it with a cake spatula. Spread the frosting on top of each of the cakes (in this cake, the tiers are not made up of several layers, just one).

E

F

G

3. Once all the tiers are covered in frosting, put them in the fridge for about 15 minutes.

4. When the frosting is cool and slightly set, use a spatula to reach under the cakes, lift them up, and assemble the 3 cakes (3 tiers each). The largest piece is placed at the bottom, followed by the middle-size, and then the smallest one. Try to center the tiers as much as possible.

5. Press the tiny colored sugar beads onto the edges of each cake tier, as well as the very bottom and where the cake tiers meet. **C**

6. Once that is done, put the cakes back in the fridge.

7. Knead the pink, blue, and white fondant a little by hand to soften it and make it uniform in texture, then roll it really thin with the rolling pin. Use the flower-shaped cutters to cut out as many small flowers as possible from the fondant. **D, E**

8. Press a tiny yellow sugar bead into the middle of each flower. This will be the center of the flower.

9. The decoration is entirely up to you. Take the cakes out of the fridge 1 at a time. Arrange the flowers on the cakes as you like, lightly pressing them into the frosting to stick. You can make flowers of any color and shape and place them anywhere on the cakes, for example, cascading just on 1 side or placing them on a different side per tier, as I did. Or even cover the whole cakes with flowers if you like! **F, G**

10. Once you are done with all 3 cakes, store them in the fridge until the big moment!

Red Velvet Cakes

Red velvet cake is the queen of all layer cakes—especially when it's coated in beautiful chocolate with a candy heart on top. When you cut these cakes and see the beautiful red inside, there's a definite wow factor. These can be a perfect gift for Valentine's Day or just to please a special someone. Share the love and spread the four cakes around to your various loved ones or blow someone away by giving them multiple cakes!

Tools & Materials

Twelve 2½-inch (6-cm) cake pans (3 pans for 1 cake)

Parchment paper

Electric mixer

Piping bags

Round decorating nozzle (about ½ inch [1.25 cm] in diameter)

Star-pattern decorating nozzle (about ¼ inch [0.6 cm] in diameter)

Cake stand (rotating optional)

Cake spatula

Heart-shaped cookie cutter (about 1½ inches [4 cm])

YIELD: 4 CAKES, ABOUT 2½ INCHES (6 CM) EACH

FOR CAKES

30 g unsalted butter, softened
75 g powdered sugar
30 g eggs (about ⅔ large egg)
15 g vegetable oil
2.5 g cocoa powder
10 g red food coloring
½ teaspoon vanilla extract
¼ teaspoon white vinegar
88 g all-purpose flour
¼ teaspoon baking soda
Pinch of salt
62 g buttermilk, room temperature

FOR FROSTING

50 g cream cheese, softened
15 g unsalted butter, softened
120 g powdered sugar
¼ teaspoon vanilla extract
10 g brown food coloring

FOR DECORATION

Sprinkles

TO MAKE THE CAKES

1. Preheat the oven to 350°F (177°C, or gas mark 4). Grease and lightly flour the cake pans or line them with parchment paper.

2. Mix the butter and sugar together in a small bowl until light in color. Add the egg gradually, beating well after each addition to combine well.

3. In a small bowl, combine the vegetable oil, cocoa powder, red food coloring, and vanilla extract until smooth. Combine this mixture with the butter mixture and stir in the vinegar.

4. In a separate bowl, sift the flour, baking soda, and salt together. Add half of the dry ingredients and half of the buttermilk to the wet ingredients, then mix well. Repeat with the remaining dry ingredients and the buttermilk.

5. Pour the batter into each of the 12 cake pans, dividing evenly. Do not fill the pans fully. Leave an inch or so empty at the top—otherwise the cakes will spill out of the pan during baking. Tap the pans on the counter 2 or 3 times to remove any air bubbles from the cakes. **A**

6. Bake them for 25 minutes or until a toothpick inserted into the center of the cakes comes out clean. Carefully remove from the oven and place on a wire rack to let cool in the pans for 15 minutes. Then, carefully remove the cakes from the cake pans and place them on the wire rack to cool completely.

A

TO MAKE THE FROSTING

1. In the small bowl of a stand mixer fitted with the paddle attachment (or in a mixing bowl using an electric mixer), beat the cream cheese until smooth. Add the butter and mix for about 30 seconds to 1 minute until well combined.

2. Mix in the powdered sugar, vanilla extract, and brown food coloring. Continue mixing until fully combined. Scrape the sides and the bottom of the bowl if needed.

B

TO ASSEMBLE THE CAKES

1. After removing from the pans, slice a thin layer off the tops of the cakes to create a flat surface. Three red cakes are needed for 1 cake. **B**

2. Fill a piping bag fitted with the round decorating nozzle with the frosting. Press a small dot of frosting in the middle of the cake stand and place the first red cake on it. Cover the top of the cake with the frosting in a circular pattern, like a snail, moving from the edges toward the center. Repeat this for all the cakes. Once that's done, use a cake spatula to spread the frosting on the sides of the cake evenly and smooth the top as well. **C**

C

D

E

F   **G**

3. Scatter some sprinkles on the bottom third of the cakes.

4. Refrigerate the cakes for 15 minutes.

5. Place a heart-shaped cookie cutter on top of each cake. Press it gently into the frosting so that it will act as a guideline. Sprinkle this heart shape on the inside, then remove the cutter carefully. **D**

6. Fit the star-pattern nozzle into the piping bag and fill it with the rest of the frosting. Pipe 12 swirls around the sprinkles heart on each cake. Put the cakes back in the fridge. **E, F**

7. Your tiny heart-decorated cakes are ready! Cut them and admire the red inside! **G**

Monster Cakes

These delicious chocolate cakes are more silly than spooky. For a Halloween party, make the Monster Cupcakes too! Just like the cupcakes, these cakes are so fun when you mix up the colors and customize the faces.

FOR CAKES

90 g all-purpose flour
5 g cocoa powder
62 g powdered sugar
¼ teaspoon baking soda
¼ teaspoon baking powder
37 g vegetable oil
62 g sour cream
30 g whole milk
½ teaspoon vanilla extract
25 g brown sugar
50 g eggs (1 large egg)
10 g dark chocolate
10 g milk chocolate
10 g ruby chocolate
5 g white fondant icing paste
5 g black fondant icing paste

FOR FROSTING

60 g unsalted butter, softened
160 g powdered sugar
15 g heavy cream
½ teaspoon vanilla extract
Food coloring: red, orange, blue, green

FOR DECORATION

Eye-shaped candy

Tools & Materials

Six 2½-inch (6-cm) cake pans (two pans for 1 cake)

Parchment paper

Electric mixer

Piping bags

Round decorating nozzle (about ½ inch [1.25 cm] in diameter)

Cake stand (rotating optional)

Cake spatula

Rolling pin

Round cookie cutters (about 1 inch [2.5 cm] in diameter and ½ inch [1.25 cm] in diameter)

Grass-pattern decorating nozzle (about ½ inch [1.25 cm] in diameter)

Star-pattern decorating nozzles (a densely serrated one and a sparsely serrated one)

YIELD: 3 CAKES, ABOUT 2½ INCHES (6 CM) EACH

TO MAKE THE CAKES

1. Preheat the oven to 350°F (177°C, or gas mark 4). Grease and lightly flour the cake pans or line them with parchment paper.

2. In a small bowl, mix the flour, cocoa powder, powdered sugar, baking soda, and baking powder.

3. Pour the vegetable oil, sour cream, milk, and vanilla extract into another small bowl, add the brown sugar and egg, and whisk to combine.

4. Add the dry ingredients to the wet ingredients and mix them using a spatula or a kitchen spoon.

5. On a cutting board, cut the dark, milk, and ruby chocolates into very small pieces. **A**

6. Divide the batter into 3 parts. Mix the dark chocolate pieces into one, the milk chocolate into another one, and the ruby chocolate into the last portion.

7. Pour the batter into each of the 6 prepared cake pans, dividing it evenly. Pour each type of batter into 2 cake pans. Do not fill the pans fully. Leave an inch or so empty at the top—otherwise, the cakes will spill out of the pan during baking. Tap the pans on the counter 2 or 3 times to remove any air bubbles from the cakes. **B**

8. Bake the cakes for 25 minutes or until a toothpick inserted into the center comes out clean. Carefully remove from the oven and place on a wire rack to let cool in the pans for 15 minutes. Then, carefully remove the cakes from the cake pans and place them back on the wire rack to cool completely.

TO MAKE THE FROSTING

1. With an electric mixer, beat the butter on medium speed until creamy. It should take about 1 minute. Add the powdered sugar, heavy cream, and vanilla extract. Beat on low speed for 30 seconds, then increase to medium-high speed and beat for 1 minute.

2. Divide the frosting into 4 parts by pouring it into 4 bowls. Color each bowl with red, orange, blue, or green food coloring until you get the desired colors.

A

B

TO ASSEMBLE THE CAKES

1. After removing from the pans, slice a thin layer off the tops of the cakes to create a flat surface, then cut them in half horizontally in the middle (just as you would cut a hamburger bun.) For 1 cake, use 2 cakes. That means 4 layers in total per cake because you've cut each cake in half. Make sure you choose identical-flavored cakes (match dark chocolate cakes together and so on). Place the 4 cakes on top of each other and cut the edges off only the top one to make a slightly round top (when filling the cakes, make sure that this remains the top cake). **C, D**

2. Choose a frosting, for example, the red one, to spread on the ruby chocolate cakes. Fill a piping bag fitted with the round decorating nozzle of ½ inch with the frosting. Press a small dot of the frosting in the middle of the cake stand and place the first matching cake on it. Cover the top of the cake with a portion of the frosting and smooth it with a cake spatula. Repeat this for all the layers of the cake. Once that's done, use a cake spatula to spread the frosting on the sides of the cakes evenly and smoothly. Put only a thin layer on the sides of the cake to allow the decorating frosting to stick (repeat for all the other cakes with all the other colored frostings). **E**

3. Refrigerate the cakes for 15 minutes.

4. Prepare the eyes and mouths. Knead the black and white fondants by hand to soften them, then roll them really thin with the rolling pin.

C

D

E

5. Cut 2 circles from the black fondant using the bigger round cookie cutter (about 1 inch [2.5 cm] in diameter). Cut 1 of them in half in the middle. These will be the mouths of your 2 monsters. Flatten the other circle a little so that it is a bit larger than 1 inch (2.5 cm). On top of this black circle, place a white circle of 1 inch (2.5 cm) and a black one on top of that that is ½ inch (1.25 cm) diameter. This will be 1 of the monster's eyes. **F**

6. Cut a circle from the white fondant using the smaller round cookie cutter (about ½ inch [1.25 cm] in diameter). Make it twice as thick as the previous ones. Place a hand-shaped black glob on it. Try to put it in the middle. This will make another monster's eye. For the third monster, use the eye-shaped candy.

TO DECORATE

1. Monster One: Take the cake covered with the red frosting out of the fridge. Fit 1 of the star-pattern nozzles in the piping bag and fill the bag with red frosting. Place a small dot of the frosting about one-third from the bottom of the cake and stick 1 of the mouths on it. Then, moving from the bottom up, cover the whole side with the frosting piped with star-pattern nozzle. Once that's done, place the thick eye you've made on top. **G**

2. Monster Two: Take the cake covered with the blue frosting out of the fridge. In a bowl, swirl the blue and orange frostings together very slightly to make a patterned frosting. Fit another star-pattern nozzle in the piping bag and fill the bag with the swirly frosting. Moving from the bottom up, cover the whole side with it. When ready, stick the big eye you've made about one-third from the top. **H**

F

G

H

3. Monster Three: Take the cake covered with the green frosting out of the fridge. Fit the grass-pattern nozzle in the piping bag and fill the bag with green frosting. Place a small dot of frosting about one-third from the bottom of the cake and stick the other mouth on it. Then, moving from the bottom up, cover the whole side with the frosting piped with the grass-pattern nozzle. When ready, stick 3 eye-shaped candies onto the frosting about one-third from the top of the cake. If you want, you can make tiny little antennas or even ears for the monsters. ∎

Your precious little monsters are ready!

Rainbow Cheesecakes

I've made a variety of mini cheesecakes, and I have to say that there's something about shrinking the standard version that makes it get lost . . . it's just too beige with the graham cracker crust and white cake. So let's jazz up the average cheesecake! These mini cheesecakes are downright captivating when you cut open the dark cookie crust to reveal layers of colorful, creamy cheesecake. Rainbow not for you? Try mixing it up with different colors. They are just as eye-catching and can be a fun way to match your treats to a baby shower theme or sports team!

FOR CRUST

45 g graham crackers, crushed

45 g chocolate wafer cookies, crushed

21 g melted unsalted butter, divided

FOR FILLING

¼ teaspoon gelatin + 28 g cold water

56 g cream cheese, softened

7 g sweetened condensed milk

5 drops of lemon juice

¼ teaspoon vanilla extract

18 g heavy cream

28 g white chocolate, melted and slightly cooled

Food coloring: pink, orange, green, blue

FOR DECORATION

48 g whipping cream

Rainbow sprinkles

Tools & Materials

Rolling pin

Four 2½-inch [6-cm] cake pans

Parchment paper

Electric mixer

Piping bag

Star-pattern decorating nozzle (about ¼ inch [0.6 cm] in diameter)

YIELD: FOUR CHEESECAKES, ABOUT 2½ INCHES (6 CM) EACH

TIP You can prepare the cheesecakes the day before they are served. They can be stored in an airtight container in the fridge for up to 3 days.

A

TO MAKE THE CRUST

1. Put the graham crackers in a sealable bag and crush them into small pieces using a rolling pin, or use a food chopper. Do the same with the chocolate wafer cookies. Add half the melted butter to each bag and combine with the crumbs. **A, B**

2. Press each crust into the bottom of 4 round cake pans lined with parchment paper and then up the sides until you have a solid crust about ¼ inch [4 mm] thick. At this tiny size, it will be a game of patience, but don't worry: The results will be great! Use the back of a spoon to smooth out and flatten each crust. When you are done, you will have 2 graham cracker crusts and 2 chocolate wafer crusts. Chill in the fridge for 30 minutes. **C**

B

TO MAKE THE FILLING

1. Add the water and gelatin to a small mixing bowl and mix until well combined. Allow to sit and soak for 5 minutes, then microwave for 15 seconds. Set aside.

2. Mix the cream cheese and condensed milk until smooth.

3. Gradually add the lemon juice and vanilla extract and mix again until smooth. Then add the heavy cream and combine until smooth. Scrape down the sides and bottom of the bowl as needed, with a spatula. Last, add the melted white chocolate and the melted gelatin. Mix until smooth.

4. Pour the mixture into 4 bowls, dividing it evenly. (You can use a kitchen scale if you have one.) Color each mixture pink, orange, green, and blue, adjusting until you have the desired shades, then mix with a spoon until they are even in color. **D**

C

5. Now, the next part is a bit time-consuming if you want each layer/color to be nice and clean and even. Begin by pouring the pink mixture into one of the prepared crusts. Place it in the freezer to chill for 10 minutes to let it set. Make sure the layer is completely frozen before adding the next layer (do not chill the colored mixture in the bowls; keep them on the countertop until ready for layering). Next add the orange layer, freeze until frozen. Repeat with the green and blue layers. **E, F**

6. Once all the layers are in the cake pans, chill in the fridge for at least 1 hour.

G

H

I

TO MAKE THE WHIPPED CREAM

1. Place the whipping cream in a small bowl and beat with a hand electric mixer until stiff peaks form. Fill a piping bag fitted with a star-pattern nozzle with the whipped cream.

2. Once the cakes are firm, gently remove from the pans and decorate them with whipped cream and rainbow sprinkles. Use a sharp knife dipped in hot water then dried to cut clean slices. Wipe the knife between each cut. **G, H, I**

Confetti-Style Birthday Cakes

Perfect for a party, this rainbow-speckled cake screams: Celebrate! A friend's or family member's birthday coming up? Surprise them with one of these tiny celebration cakes. They'll be so happy. Make them with a frosting as colorful as possible and decorate with rainbow sprinkles. Again, the only limit is your imagination! You'll even color the cakes too!

FOR CAKES
56 g all-purpose flour
¼ teaspoon baking powder
¼ teaspoon baking soda
Pinch of salt
37 g granulated sugar
56 g unsalted butter, softened
¼ teaspoon vanilla extract
50 g eggs (1 large egg)
52 g whole milk
25 g rainbow sprinkles

FOR FROSTING
62 g unsalted butter, softened
125 g powdered sugar
¼ teaspoon vanilla extract
Food coloring: pink, yellow

FOR GANACHE
28 g white chocolate
31 g heavy cream
Food coloring: blue
Rainbow sprinkles

Tools & Materials
Twelve 2½-inch (6-cm) cake pans (3 pans for 1 cake)
Electric mixer
Cake stand (rotating optional)
Cake spatula
Piping bag
Star-pattern decorating nozzle (about ¼ inch [0.6 cm] in diameter)
Candles

YIELD: 4 CAKES, ABOUT 2½ INCHES (6 CM) EACH

TO MAKE THE CAKES

1. Preheat the oven to 350°F (177°C, or gas mark 4). Grease and lightly flour the cake pans or line them with parchment paper.

2. Sift the flour in a small bowl and whisk it together with the baking powder, baking soda, and salt. Set aside.

3. In a separate small bowl, combine the sugar, butter, and vanilla extract and beat with an electric mixer until pale and fluffy (about 5 minutes on high speed for most mixers). Scrape the sides and the bottom of the bowl with a rubber spatula if needed. Add the egg gradually, beating after each addition until fully incorporated.

4. With the mixer on low speed, add the dry ingredients to the wet ingredients in 3 additions, alternating with the milk. Mix until you have a smooth cake batter. Do not overmix.

5. Add the rainbow sprinkles and fold them into the batter with a spatula, not an electric mixer. Pour the batter into each cake pan, dividing it evenly. Do not fill the pans fully. Leave an inch or so empty from the top—otherwise the cakes will spill out of the pan during baking. **A**

6. Bake for around 25 minutes or until the cakes are baked thoroughly. To test for doneness, insert a toothpick into the center of the cake. If it comes out clean, it is done.

7. Let the cakes cool completely in the pans on a wire rack. The cakes must be completely cool to continue working with them!

TO MAKE THE FROSTING

1. To make the frosting, place the butter in a small bowl and beat with a hand electric mixer until fluffy. Sift the powdered sugar on top and combine together at low speed, then beat at high speed for a few minutes until the mixture is pale and fluffy. It should take about 2 minutes. Add the vanilla extract and beat again to combine.

2. Transfer three-quarters (almost all) of the frosting to a separate bowl and add a dash of pink food coloring to it. Mix and add more coloring if necessary until the desired shade is achieved. (You will fill the cake and coat the outside with the pink frosting.) To the rest of the frosting, add a dash of yellow food coloring. (This will be used to make the swirls at the top of the cake.)

B

C

TO ASSEMBLE THE CAKES

1. Using a large serrated knife, slice a thin layer off of the tops of the cakes to create a flat surface.

2. Put a small amount of frosting onto the cake platter and place one of the cakes on top.

3. Evenly cover the top of the cake with the pink frosting. Top with the second cake and evenly cover the top of that one with the frosting. Gently rock the palette knife back and forth to disperse the frosting and turn the turntable in the opposite direction to which you are spreading. Finish with the third cake layer and spread the remaining pink frosting all over the top and the sides of the cake. Scrape the excess frosting off the sides of the cake using the side scraper. Repeat until you have a nice and smooth finish. **B, C**

4. Scatter some sprinkles on the bottom third of the cake. You can choose the sprinkles you put in the cake or more colorful ones. Repeat with the other 3 cakes. **D**

5. Put the cake in the fridge for 20 to 30 minutes or until you finish making the ganache.

TO MAKE THE GANACHE

1. Cut the white chocolate into really small pieces of about ¼ inch (0.6 cm) on a cutting board and place in a small heat-proof bowl.

2. In a saucepan over medium-high heat, warm the whipping cream until it just starts to simmer, whisking constantly. I always look for small bubbles forming around the edge and a soft boil starting in the middle. When it reaches this stage, pour the cream over the white chocolate.

D

3. Whisk together until the ganache has the same consistency all around and there are no bits of chocolate left on your whisk.

4. Add a few drops of blue food coloring to the ganache until you get the desired color.

5. Once you've whisked the ganache, it's crucial to let it cool on the countertop until it's room temperature. It takes about 20 to 30 minutes depending on how cold your environment is.

6. When the frosting on your cake is chilled, do a test drip by letting the ganache run down the side of your cake. If it trickles rapidly and pools at the bottom, your ganache is too warm. Continue to cool the ganache for another 5 to 10 minutes and try your test drip again. If it's lumpy or doesn't trickle very far down the side of the cake, it's too cold. Reheat the ganache in the microwave for about 10 seconds, stir, and try again. Repeat the reheating process as needed until you get the perfect consistency. **E**

7. When the consistency of the ganache has become satisfactory, it's best to drip the sides of the cake before filling in the top. Try to use as little as possible on the top and spread it out. Don't worry: It will have a nice smooth surface!

8. Beat the rest of the yellow frosting and place it into a piping bag fitted with the star-pattern nozzle (use a small star-pattern tube of about ¼ inch [about 0.6 cm] in diameter). Pipe 8 swirls on top of the cake and sprinkle them with the remaining sprinkles, or choose larger sugar balls and place one at the top of each swirl. You can decorate the yellow swirls with anything you like. **F, G**

9. Choose some nice candles to stick in the middle of the cake. If you can't find tiny candles, you can cut larger candles carefully and voilà, you've got a tiny candle!

E

F

G

Animal Cakes

Let's make a whole zoo! Are you ready? Trust me, it's not that complicated. The Confetti-Style Birthday Cakes recipe is the jumping-off point. You'll follow those instructions and only the decorations are different. I'll show you how to make a giraffe, a cat, and a dragon. By the end, I think you'll get the hang of it, and you can swap colors and features to make other animals as well (maybe a cute little dog or mouse?).

Tools & Materials

Nine 2½-inch (6-cm) cake pans (3 pans for 1 cake)

Electric mixer

Cake stand (rotating optional)

Cake spatula

YIELD: 3 CAKES, ABOUT 2½ INCHES (6 CM) EACH

FOR CAKES

See recipe for Confetti-Style Birthday Cakes, page 63.

FOR FROSTING

See recipe for Confetti-Style Birthday Cakes, page 63.
Food coloring: yellow, green, purple

FOR DECORATION

15 g fondant icing paste
Food coloring: brown, black, white, yellow, purple, blue, pink

TO MAKE THE CAKES

1. Follow steps 1-7 for the Confetti-Style Birthday Cakes recipe.

2. Let cakes cool completely.

TO FROST THE CAKES

1. Complete the first step for making the frosting in the Confetti-Style Birthday Cakes recipe.

2. Divide the frosting into 3 portions and color them yellow, green, and purple with food coloring.

3. Frost each cake per the directions of the Confetti-Style Birthday Cakes and put them in the fridge for 20 to 30 minutes.

A

B

C

D

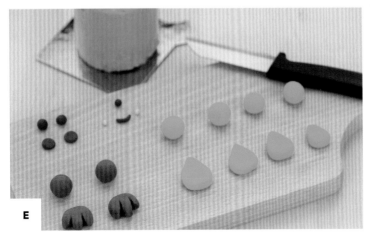

E

F

TO ASSEMBLE THE GIRAFFE CAKE

1. Divide the fondant icing paste into 3 portions. (You will use 5 g of the icing paste per cake.) Divide the 5 g for the giraffe cake in half. Color one-half brown. Divide the other half into 3 more portions and color them black, white, and yellow.

2. Using the yellow paste, make 2 circles about ½ inch (2.5 cm) in diameter. Shape this into the ears of the giraffe (see photo). **A**

3. Prepare the eyes and mouth using the black and white paste.

4. Shape the face and little horns from the brown paste and the spots for the body too. Use the photos as a guideline.

5. Take the cake with the yellow frosting out of the fridge. Place the horns at the top of the cake and the ears next to them. Place the cheeks on the sides/bottom of the cake and the 2 eyes above them. Scatter the spots all over its body. **B**

Your first animal is ready!

TO ASSEMBLE THE CAT CAKE

1. Divide 5 g of the fondant icing paste in half. Color one-half dark purple. Divide the other half into 3 more portions and color them black, white, and light purple.

2. Form the darker purple paste into 3 balls of about ½ inch (1.25 cm) in diameter. Flatten out two of them to make ears, and shape 1 of them into a face (see photo). Use this color to create spots on the body too. **C**

3. Form the lighter purple paste into 2 balls of about ¼ inch (0.6 cm) in diameter. Flatten them out and place them onto the darker purple circles. The ears are ready.

4. With the black paste, make the nose and the eyes. Place little dots on the eyes using the white paste.

5. Take the cake with the purple frosting out of the fridge. Place the ears at the top/sides of the cake. Place the cheeks and the black nose on the sides/bottom of the cake and the 2 eyes above them. Scatter the spots all over its body. **D**

Your kitten is all done! You have two cakes ready. One more to go. Are you ready?

TO ASSEMBLE THE DRAGON CAKE

1. Divide 5 g of the fondant icing paste in half. Color one-half green. Divide the other half into 4 more portions and color them black, white, light blue, and light pink.

2. Form the green paste into 5 balls of about ½ inch (1.25 cm) in diameter. Flatten 3 of them and shape them into triangles to make the dragon's crest and the other 2 to make its legs. **E**

3. Form the light pink paste into 2 balls of about ¼ inch (0.6 cm) in diameter. Flatten them out to make the blush of the cheeks.

4. Prepare the eyes using the black, white, and light blue pastes.

5. Prepare a tiny black mouth. (Remember to use the photos as a guide for all the decorations!)

6. Take the cake with the green frosting out of the fridge. Place the 3 crests at the top of the cake. Place the cheeks and the black nose on the sides/bottom of the cake and the 2 eyes above them. For the eyes, first place the white flat circle, then the blue one, and last, the black one. Finally, the legs go at the bottom. **F**

Have you ever seen such a "scary" dragon?

4

Cookies

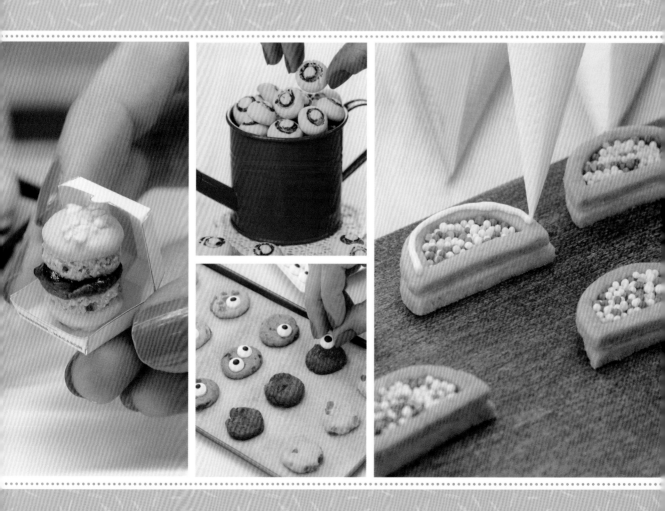

Chocolate Mint Cookies

I didn't think I could love mint cookies any more than I already did—and then I tried these little turtle cookies! Something about the shape and the green color just made them even tastier. You're never too old to enjoy animal cookies, I say! If you're afraid of too much mint flavor, feel free to use a little less extract in your first batch . . . though, of course, I think the level of mint I recommend is perfect.

Tools & Materials

Small baking sheet
Parchment paper
Electric mixer

YIELD: 7 COOKIES

FOR COOKIES

28 g unsalted butter, softened
28 g brown sugar
18 g eggs (about ⅓ large egg)
¼ teaspoon vanilla extract
40 g all-purpose flour
¼ teaspoon baking powder
Pinch of salt
5 g cacao powder
Food coloring: green
¼ teaspoon mint extract

FOR DECORATION

5 g white fondant icing paste
Black food coloring pen

TO MAKE THE COOKIES

1. Preheat the oven to 350°F (177°C, or gas mark 4) and line a baking sheet with parchment paper.

2. In a small bowl, beat the butter and sugar until creamy, about 2 minutes. Add the egg and vanilla extract and beat until combined, about 1 minute. Scrape down the sides and bottom of the bowl as needed while mixing.

3. On low speed, beat in the flour, baking powder, and salt until the dough forms. Divide the dough in half.

4. To one-half, add the cacao powder. To the other half, add the green food coloring and mint extract. Mix until blended. Wrap both doughs in plastic wrap and refrigerate for at least 30 minutes.

TO MAKE THE TURTLES

1. Use the green dough to make the body of the turtle. The brown one will be the shell. Let's start with the body.

2. Make a lot of balls, smaller than ½ inch (about 0.6 cm), from the green dough. You will need 5 balls for 1 turtle. Make 4 balls slightly oblong and flatten them. These will be the legs. Attach them together, leaving room for the head. **A**

3. Once that's done, prepare the body. Take the brown dough and make a circle of about 1 inch (2.5 cm). Flatten it a little and use a knife to carve the top as if it was chequered. Place it on the green legs. **B**

4. Make as many turtles as you can with the dough. Put them on a baking sheet.

5. Bake for 11 to 12 minutes or until the edges appear to set and are lightly browned.

6. Remove from the oven and allow the cookies to cool on the baking sheet for 2 minutes.

7. Then transfer to a wire rack to cool completely.

8. Make little eyes using the fondant icing paste. (You can find the preparation method in the Frog Cake Pops recipe, page 31.) **C**

9. If you'd like, draw mouths with the black food coloring pen.

They will turn out charming!

A

B

C

Rainbow Cookies

While the look of these cookies may steal the show, don't let that distract you from the true showstopper: These cookies contain the recipe for the best-ever sugar cookie icing! Try it and I think you'll be converted as well. Okay, back to the design: Once you master the recipe, make the cookies unique with a complementary sprinkle design or even a little message inside.

Tools & Materials

Electric mixer

Small baking sheet

Parchment paper

Rolling pin

Piping bags

Round cookie cutters
  (about 1 inch [2.5 cm] or
  1½ inches [4 cm] in diameter)

YIELD: 25 COOKIES

FOR COOKIES

57 g unsalted butter, softened
20 g granulated sugar
15 g eggs (about ⅓ large egg)
¼ teaspoon vanilla extract
90 g all-purpose flour
Pinch of salt

FOR ICING

50 g powdered sugar
10 g egg whites (about
  ⅓ egg white)
¼ teaspoon cornstarch
Food coloring: red, orange,
  yellow, green, blue

FOR DECORATION

Sprinkles

TIP For the cookie recipes, you can freeze some of the dough if you don't want to use it all, but all these cookies are guaranteed to go fast!

TO PREPARE THE COOKIES

1. Beat the butter and sugar together in a small bowl with an electric mixer until light and fluffy.

2. Beat the egg, then stir in the vanilla extract and add both to the butter mixture. Combine the flour and salt in a separate bowl, add to the butter mixture, and mix to form a dough.

3. Cover the dough with plastic wrap and chill for at least 1 hour.

4. Preheat the oven to 350°F (177°C, or gas mark 4) and line a baking sheet with parchment paper.

A

5. Roll out the cookie dough to paper-thin. Use the cookie cutter to cut out circles. Cut the circles in halves. You will need 3 semicircles for 1 cookie. Two semicircles will be "full," but cut a hole in the middle of the third one. Leave a thin border and cut out the center with a knife. Place the cookies on the baking sheet. **A, B**

6. Bake them in the oven until lightly golden at the edges, about 8 to 10 minutes. Transfer the cookies to a wire rack to cool.

TO MAKE THE ICING

1. Sift the powdered sugar into a small bowl.

2. Add the egg white and cornstarch and combine with a wooden spoon.

3. When you have a nice thick paste, mix it with an electric mixer on medium speed until you get a stiff consistency. It is good if it does not drip off the whisk.

B

4. Divide the icing into 5 portions and color each with food coloring (red, orange, yellow, blue, green), 1 color for each portion. Put each icing in separate piping bags. Use a small amount at a time, as it is much easier to work with. Cover the rest so that it does not dry out.

5. Tie the big end of the piping bag tightly so that the icing will not run back. Using scissors, cut a very small hole at the tip of the disposable piping bag.

6. Arrange the cookies in groups of 3. Two semicircles are "full" and the third has a hole in the middle. Draw a rainbow on 1 of the full semicircles, as you can see in the photo. Move inward from the outside. Once you have applied a color, wait until it has set a little and then apply the next one. The order is red, orange, yellow, green, and blue. **C**

C

D   E

F

7. Take the other full semicircle and draw a strip of icing around the edge. Place the semicircle with the hole on top of it so that it sticks. Then drizzle sprinkles into the hole or write a special message and put it in folded. Then draw a strip of icing on the edge of the half circle with the hole and stick the top semicircle with the rainbow on top. **D, E, F**

And there you go!
Break a cookie in half and let the
sugar seep out! Delicious!

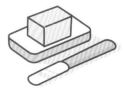

Monster Cookies

Are you ready for the trifecta? You've seen the Monster Cupcakes (page 15) and Monster Cakes (page 53)— now it's time for Monster Cookies! Gooey monster cookies are great all year long. (After all, don't we all have our own little monster at home who loves cookies?!) As always, I encourage monster madness by making these in many colors and with many face variations. And since this recipe makes more than 28 cookies, it's also great for a cookie-decorating party!

FOR COOKIES

28 g unsalted butter, softened

28 g brown sugar

18 g eggs (about ⅓ large egg)

1 teaspoon whole milk

¼ teaspoon vanilla extract

½ teaspoon almond extract

40 g all-purpose flour

Pinch of salt

¼ teaspoon baking soda

Food coloring: red, yellow, blue, green

5 maraschino cherries

Pinch of salt

FOR DECORATION

Eye-shaped candy

TO MAKE THE COOKIES

1. Preheat the oven to 350°F (177°C, or gas mark 4) and line a baking sheet with parchment paper.

2. In a small bowl, beat the butter until creamy, about 2 minutes. Add the brown sugar, then beat for about 2 more minutes. Add the egg and beat until combined, about 1 minute. Scrape down the sides and bottom of the bowl as needed while mixing. Add the milk, vanilla extract, and almond extract and beat until combined.

3. In a separate small bowl, thoroughly whisk the flour, salt, and baking soda. Then stir the dry ingredients into the butter mixture with an electric mixer. The dough will be very creamy and soft.

4. Cover and chill the cookie dough in the fridge for at least 1 to 2 hours, and up to 3 days.

5. Cut the cherries into small pieces. Make them real small.

6. Divide the chilled dough into 4 portions. Add 1 food color to each batch, then mix in 28 g cherries into each portion.

7. Make balls of about ½ inch (1.25 cm) and put them on the baking sheet about 1 inch (2.5 cm) apart. Flatten each ball with your fingers. The disks should not touch each other. **A**

8. Place the eye-shaped candies on top randomly. **B**

9. Bake for 10 minutes, or until the edges appear to set and are lightly browned. The centers will still look soft.

10. Remove from the oven and allow the cookies to cool on the baking sheet for 2 minutes. After 2 minutes, transfer to a wire rack to cool completely.

A

B

"Burger" Cookies

They're burgers . . . wait, they're cookies . . . wait, they're sweet sandwich cookies that look like mini burgers! What a fun treat for the summer BBQ season. Bring them to a cookout, a pool party, or a birthday celebration for your favorite grillmaster. It is, of course, easiest to make them as-is, but if you're feeling creative, you can try to customize the toppings. Thin slices of dried coconut without any dye could stand in as onion, for example!

Tools & Materials

Electric mixer
Small baking sheet
Parchment paper
Rolling pin
Piping bags

YIELD: 30 COOKIES

FOR COOKIES

40 g unsalted butter, softened
25 g brown sugar
20 g egg yolks (yolk from
    1 large egg)
¼ teaspoon vanilla extract
1 banana
66 g all-purpose flour
Pinch of salt

Sesame seeds
10 g oat flakes
5 g cacao powder

FOR DECORATION

10 g shredded coconut
Food coloring: green, red, yellow
50 g white chocolate callets

TO PREPARE THE COOKIES

1. Using an electric mixer, beat the butter and sugar together in a small bowl until light and fluffy.

2. Next, add the egg yolk and vanilla extract to the butter mixture. Whisk well to combine.

3. Mash the banana with a fork, then add to the butter mixture. Mix well to combine.

4. Add the flour and salt.

5. Divide the batter into 3 portions. Mix 2 portions again. These will make your hamburger "buns." Form balls of about ½ inch (1.25 cm) in diameter. Place them on a baking sheet lined with parchment paper at an even distance and flatten them a little. Sprinkle sesame seeds on every second flattened ball. These will be the top buns.

6. Mix in the oat flakes and cacao powder to the rest of the dough. These will make the hamburger "patties." Form balls of about ½ inch (1.25 cm) in diameter, place on the baking sheet, and flatten. **A**

A

B

7. Place the baking sheet in the fridge while preheating the oven.

8. Preheat the oven to 350°F (177°C, or gas mark 4).

9. Bake until lightly golden at the edges, about 8 to 10 minutes. Transfer the cookies to a wire rack to cool.

TO DECORATE

1. Place the shredded coconut in a small resealable plastic bag and add some green food coloring. Shake well until the food coloring has absorbed and turned the coconut green. **B**

2. Melt the white chocolate (see any cake pop recipe, pages 27-42), then color half the chocolate red (imitation ketchup) and half yellow (imitation mustard). Pour each into a piping bag. (You can use frosting instead of melted chocolate if you'd like.)

C

3. Turn the hamburger "buns" upside down. Pipe a circle of the yellow chocolate onto the bottom layer. Place the brown cookie onto it. Pipe the red and yellow chocolate on top of the cookie, sprinkle it with green shredded coconut, then place the bun with sesame seeds on top. **C, D**

4. Repeat this process with all the cookies.

Don't they look like real burgers?

D

Peanut Butter Cereal Cookies

The base dough for this recipe used to be what I thought of as the best peanut butter cookies ever. Well, they were until one day I hit on a way to make them even better: Just add cereal. That's right: Breakfast cereals can do more than taste good in a bowl of milk . . . you can bake with them! Let's make some very colorful and tasty cookies with cereal mix-ins.

Tools & Materials

Small baking sheet

Parchment paper

YIELD: 80 COOKIES, ABOUT ½ INCH (1.25 CM) EACH

FOR COOKIES

28 g unsalted butter, softened
28 g brown sugar
25 g granulated sugar
18 g eggs (about ⅓ large egg)
11 g peanut butter
¼ teaspoon vanilla extract
40 g all-purpose flour
¼ teaspoon baking soda
¼ teaspoon baking powder
Pinch of salt

4 types of cereals (See the photos for what kinds of cereals you can use. The more colorful the flakes, the more interesting the cookies will look. If necessary, cut cereal flakes into smaller pieces!)

TO MAKE THE COOKIES

1. Preheat the oven to 350°F (177°C, or gas mark 4) and line a baking sheet with parchment paper.

2. In a small bowl, beat the butter until creamy, about 2 minutes. Add the brown sugar and granulated sugar, then beat for about 2 more minutes. Add the egg and beat until combined, about 1 minute. Scrape down the sides and bottom of the bowl as needed while mixing. Add the peanut butter and vanilla extract and beat until combined.

3. In a separate small bowl, thoroughly whisk together the flour, baking soda, baking powder, and salt. Then stir the dry ingredients into the butter mixture. The dough will be very creamy and soft. **A**

4. Cover and chill the cookie dough in the fridge for at least 1 to 2 hours, and up to 3 days.

5. Divide the chilled dough into 4 portions, or as many kinds of cereal you want to put in. Knead a small amount of cereal into each portion of dough.

6. Make balls of about ½ inch (1.25 cm) and put them on a baking sheet about 1 inch (2.5 cm) apart. Flatten each ball with your fingers. The disks should not touch each other. **B**

7. Bake for 11 to 12 minutes, or until the edges appear to set and are lightly browned. The centers will still look soft.

8. Remove from the oven and allow the cookies to cool on the baking sheet for 2 minutes. After 2 minutes, transfer to a wire rack to cool completely. They will stay fresh at room temperature in a tightly covered container for up to a week.

Be careful: Once you taste them, you won't be able to stop eating them.

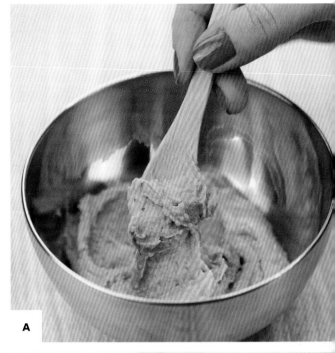

A

B

Electric mixer

Small baking sheet

Parchment paper

Drinking straw

YIELD: 50 COOKIES, ABOUT
½ INCH (1.25 CM) EACH

Mushroom-Lover Cookies

Prank someone with mushroom-shaped cookies or give these to the mushroom lover in your life. Either way, these sweet button mushroom–inspired cookies will put a smile on someone's face. They are delicious, crumbly, and very cute. They are also quick and easy to make. The hardest part is finding the perfect little basket or tin to serve them in.

FOR COOKIES

30 g unsalted butter, softened
20 g powdered sugar
15 g eggs (about ⅓ large egg)
¼ teaspoon vanilla extract
45 g all-purpose flour

22.5 g cornstarch
¼ teaspoon baking powder
1 tablespoon cocoa powder
Powdered sugar

TO MAKE THE COOKIES

1. Preheat the oven to 375°F (190°C, or gas mark 5).

2. In a small bowl, beat the butter and sugar with an electric mixer until creamy. Add the egg and vanilla extract and beat until combined.

3. Stir in the flour, cornstarch, and baking powder with a wooden spoon first, then mix or knead by hand until a soft dough forms. The dough should not stick to your hands. Add more flour if necessary.

4. Place the dough onto a table (or countertop) sprinkled with flour and spread out evenly—you will get a playdough-like consistency, soft and pleasant.

5. Cut it into small pieces with a small knife and make tiny balls smaller than ½ inch (about 1.25 cm) by hand. Place them on a baking sheet lined with parchment paper. **A**

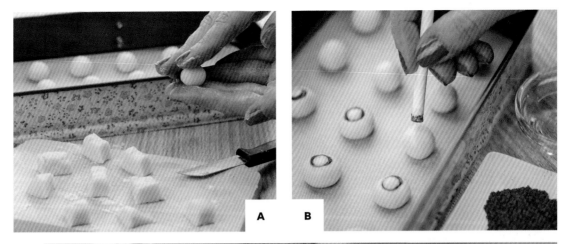

6. Put the cocoa powder on a small flat plate. Take a straw and dip 1 end into water, but only the tip, and then into the cocoa powder. Gently press the straw into each ball of dough (at about ¹⁄₁₀-inch [2.5-mm] depth) and remove carefully. This is how the pattern and the stem of the mushroom are formed. Make sure you do not flatten the balls! **B**

7. Bake for 12 to 15 minutes. Be careful not to let them get too brown.

8. Remove from the oven and cool on a wire rack. Sprinkle with powdered sugar if desired. **C**

9. Store them in an airtight container with the lid slightly open for up to a week.

"Burger" Macarons

Who doesn't love burgers? And macarons? Everybody, of course! How about combining the two and creating "burger" macarons? They're so cute, you will not want to ruin them by eating them. But I promise you: They are delicious.

FOR MACARONS

31 g almond flour
63 g powdered sugar
31 g egg whites (about 1 egg white from 1 large egg)
17.5 g granulated sugar
1 teaspoon sesame seeds

FOR FILLING

29 g unsalted butter, softened
57 g powdered sugar
¼ teaspoon vanilla extract

Pinch of salt
28 g chocolate-hazelnut spread
3 g cocoa powder
10 g heavy cream

FOR DECORATION

Green gummy candy (for the "lettuce")
Strawberry or raspberry jam (for the "ketchup")

Tools & Materials

Paper

Pen

Parchment paper

Food processor

Fine mesh sieve

Electric mixer

Silicone spatula

Small baking sheet

Piping bags

Round decorating nozzle (about ¼ inch [0.6 cm] in diameter)

YIELD: 30 MACARONS, ABOUT 1 TO 1½ INCHES (2.5 TO 4 CM) EACH

TO MAKE THE MACARON SHELLS

A

1. Draw circles of about ½ inch (1.25 cm) on a piece of paper, a little bit more than 1 inch (2.5 cm) apart from each other. Place the paper in a small baking sheet, then place a piece of white parchment paper on top to make the pattern transparent.

2. Combine the almond flour and powdered sugar in a food processor and pulse a few times until well blended. Sift through a fine mesh sieve. Set aside.

3. In a small bowl, with an electric mixer, beat the egg white and sugar on high speed for about 6 minutes, until stiff peaks form. **A**

4. Add the almond flour and sugar mixture to the egg white and start folding it into the egg white, using a silicone spatula. Fold, scraping the sides of the bowl and trying to deflate the meringue and incorporating the dry ingredients into it at the same time. Continue folding until the batter is thick and glossy. When you pick some batter up with the spatula and drop it into the bowl, it should settle into the rest within 15 to 20 seconds.

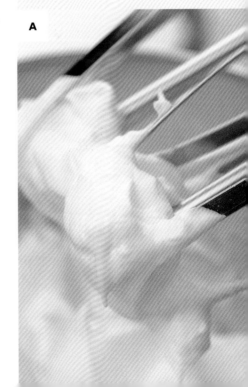

5. Cut the tip of a piping bag and fit a small (about ¼ inch [about 0.6 cm] in diameter) round nozzle into the slot. Fill the piping bag with the batter.

6. Hold the piping bag vertically to the baking sheet, with the nozzle about ½ inch (1.25 cm) from it. Place the tip of the nozzle in the center of the circle you have drawn (the tip shouldn't touch the paper) and press out the batter until it fully covers the circle. Don't lift the tip of the nozzle until you have fully made a circle to avoid a hollow macaron shell. When lifting the bag, stop pressing the batter. **B**

7. Gently tap the baking sheet (with the macaron circles on it) on the counter six times. This will let any air bubbles out. Sprinkle sesame seeds on top of half of the circles (if you have six circles, sprinkle only 3). This will make the top halves of the hamburger "buns."

8. Allow the macarons to form a skin by letting them sit at room temperature for 30 minutes or longer.

9. Preheat the oven to 325°F (163°C, or gas mark 3). Bake the macaron shells for 10 to 12 minutes, until set but not browned. If they brown very quickly, you might need to turn the oven temperature down.

10. Transfer the baking sheet to a wire rack and let the shells cool completely.

11. Peel the shells off the parchment paper and turn the shells that don't have sesame seeds on them upside down. Be careful not to break them.

B

C

D

TO MAKE THE FILLING

1. In a small bowl, with a hand mixer, whisk the butter and half of the powdered sugar on medium-high speed until fluffy, about 3 to 4 minutes. Be sure it's completely smooth before adding more sugar.

2. Add the vanilla extract and salt and mix thoroughly.

3. Add the chocolate-hazelnut spread, cocoa powder, and heavy cream. Beat on low speed for 30 seconds, then increase to medium-high speed and beat for 2 minutes. It may seem to be curdling at first, but keep beating and it will come together. (If the mixture is too thick, you can add more heavy cream.)

4. Pour the chocolate cream into the piping bag with a round nozzle. Line up the hamburger macaron bottoms (the ones without sesame seeds). The flat half should face up. Press a layer of imitation "meat" (a.k.a. your chocolate cream) on top. **C**

5. Cut the green gummy candy into really thin slices. Place them on top of your chocolate cream, overhanging the edge a little.

6. Add the strawberry or raspberry jam to a piping bag. Cut a very tiny hole in it and press a little red jam over your chocolate cream and gummy candy, just like ketchup. Then put the top bun on your "hamburger." **D**

Voilà! You now have a full "burger" macaron!

5

Pies

Apple Pies

Let's make a classic apple pie together! My grandma used to make these (at normal size!), and I always loved the smell of freshly baked pie—and the taste of the crumbly crust falling apart in my mouth, melding with the apples and cinnamon. Serve this miniature version warm or cold and with whipped cream or tiny, tiny scoops of vanilla ice cream. It might go without saying, but these make everyone smile if you bring them out as a surprise for Thanksgiving or Christmas dessert!

FOR CRUST

28 g unsalted butter
70 g all-purpose flour
¼ teaspoon salt
½ teaspoon sugar
30 g full-fat sour cream

FOR FILLING

1 apple
11 g unsalted butter
6 g all-purpose flour
23 g granulated sugar
1 g cinnamon
Pinch of lemon zest

FOR BRUSHING

19 g egg yolks (yolk from
    1 large egg)

TO MAKE THE CRUST

1. Cut the butter into cubes and let them sit on a plate so that they're not freezing cold, but they shouldn't warm up!

2. In a small bowl, vigorously whisk the flour, salt, and sugar.

3. Places the cubes of butter into the flour mixture. Use clean hands to squish the flour and butter together with your fingers, then your knuckles.

4. Add the sour cream and use a fork to incorporate it into the mixture. You now have pie dough!

5. Place the pie dough on a lightly floured work surface (for example, a table). Using floured hands, fold the dough into itself until the flour is fully incorporated. Form it into a ball. Don't worry about overworking this dough. Just form it so that there are no cracks in it.

Tools & Materials

Five baking pans (2 ½ inches [6 cm] in diameter)

Rolling pin

Plastic wrap

YIELD: 5 PIES, ABOUT 2½ INCHES (6 CM) EACH

TIP If you use store-bought dough, you will need to roll it to about one-third the thickness (in other words, it comes in a thickness better suited to a "normal" pie than mini pies!).

6. Divide the dough in 2 halves and flatten into 2 disks. Sprinkle them all over with a little flour. Wrap tightly with plastic wrap and refrigerate for at least 2 hours.

7. After the dough has chilled, it's time to roll it out. Keep a small bowl of flour nearby to keep your work surface, rolling pin, and hands lightly floured. This prevents the pie dough from sticking. When rolling the pie dough out, always start from the center and work your way out in all directions, turning the dough as you go.

8. Smooth out the edges if you notice cracks. (If the dough feels too warm or the butter inside is melting, stop and chill the dough in the fridge for at least 10 minutes before continuing.)

9. From half of the dough, stretch 5 disks about 3½ inches (9 cm) in diameter for the 2½-inch (6-cm)-diameter baking pans. Take each rolled-out disk in your hands and place it on a baking pan. Using your fingers, gently start to press in the center to reach the bottom of the pan and then press the edges. Make sure the dough does not tear or warm up! Use your fingers to make the edges of the pies slightly wavy. Put them in the fridge while you make the pie filling. **A**

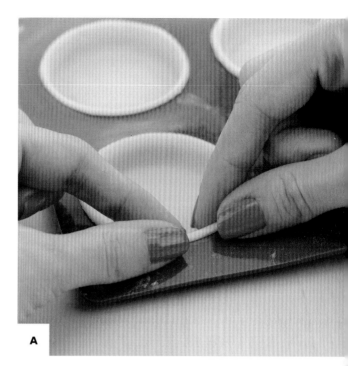

A

TO MAKE THE FILLING

1. Peel and core the apple, then slice it real thin. Set aside.

2. Melt the butter in a saucepan over medium heat. Add the flour and stir until a thick paste forms. Add the sugar, cinnamon, and lemon zest and cook for about 1 more minute. Stir continuously. Remove from the heat. Set it aside to cool down a bit.

3. Dry the sliced apple slices with a paper towel and roll them in the cinnamon-sugar mixture. Mix and spoon into the pie crusts. **B**

B

C

D

TO MAKE THE PIES

1. Roll out the other half of the dough and cut strips of ¼ inch (0.6 cm) thick and about 3 inches (8 cm) long. **C**

2. Lay 5 strips vertically and evenly spaced over the top of each filled pie.

3. Fold the first and third strips all the way back so that they're almost falling off the pie. Lay 1 of the unused strips perpendicular over the second and fourth strips, then unfold the first and third strips back into their original position. **D**

4. Fold the second and fourth vertical strips back. Lay 1 of the 3 unused strips perpendicular over top. Unfold the first and third strips back into their original position. **E**

5. Repeat steps 15 and 16 to weave in the last 2 strips of dough. Fold and trim excess dough at the edges as necessary and pinch to secure.

6. Brush the top of each crust with egg yolk.

7. Position an oven rack in the lower third of the oven, then place a baking sheet on the oven rack to catch any drips from the pies as they are baking.

8. Preheat the oven to 400°F (205°C, or gas mark 6).

9. Bake the pies on top of the hot baking sheet for 10 minutes, reduce the heat to 350°F (177°C, or gas mark 4), then continue to bake for 10 to 15 minutes, or until the crust is golden and the juices in the filling are bubbling.

10. If the crust begins to overbrown, cover the edges of the pies with aluminum foil and continue to bake until done. Let the pies cool for 1 hour before cutting to allow the filling to set.

E

KEEPING PIE DOUGH COLD

Why is it important for the pie dough to be cold? The butter in the pie dough will melt in the oven. Butter has a high volume of water content, and this water converts to steam as the pie dough is baking. The steam separates the dough into multiple flaky layers, making this the most delicious pie crust ever. The colder the dough, the flakier the pie crust will be.

Three tips to keep pie dough cold:

1. Use ice-cold water.

2. Use cold sour cream.

3. Chill the pie dough for at least 2 hours before rolling out.

Strawberry Pies

Have you ever seen such a pink, flowery pie? I know, it's not your ordinary pie (even by this book's standards!), but it is surprisingly easy to make. Beautiful and divinely delicious, this pie makes for a memorable treat no matter what—or whom—you bake it for.

FOR CRUST
100 g store-bought dough or
    homemade dough (see the
    Apple Pies recipe, page 95)
Food coloring: green, red

FOR FILLING
75 g strawberries
21 g granulated sugar
½ teaspoon cornstarch
¼ teaspoon vanilla extract
5 teaspoons water

FOR BRUSHING
19 g egg yolks (yolk from
    1 large egg)

Tools & Materials

5 baking pans (2½ inches
    [6 cm] in diameter)

Rolling pin

Plastic wrap

Round cookie cutters: about
    1 inch (2.5 cm) in diameter,
    ½ inch (1.25 cm), and ¼ inch
    (0.6 cm)

Small leaf-shaped cookie
    cutters

Small flower-shaped cookie
    cutters

**YIELD: 5 PIES, ABOUT
2½ INCHES (6 CM) EACH**

TO PREPARE THE CRUSTS

1. Cut off one-sixth of the dough. Cut it in half and color one half with green food coloring until you get the desired color, and the other half with bright red food coloring. Wrap them in plastic wrap.

2. Paint the remaining dough with red food coloring, but only do so to get a pale pink color. Divide this dough into 2 halves and flatten into 2 disks. Sprinkle them all over with a little flour. Wrap tightly with plastic wrap and refrigerate for at least 2 hours. **A**

3. After the dough has chilled, it's time to roll it out. Keep a small bowl of flour nearby to keep your work surface, rolling pin, and hands lightly floured. This prevents the pie dough from sticking. When rolling the pie dough out, always start from the center and work your way out in all directions, turning the dough as you go.

4. Smooth out the edges if you notice cracks. (If the pie dough feels too warm or the butter inside is melting, stop and chill the dough in the fridge for at least 10 minutes before continuing.)

TIP If you use store-bought dough, you will need to roll it to about one-third the thickness (in other words, it comes in a thickness better suited to a "normal" pie than mini pies!).

A

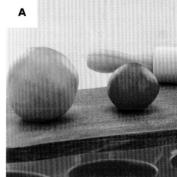

5. From half of the dough, stretch 5 disks about 3½ inches (9 cm) in diameter for the 2½-inch (6-cm)-diameter baking pans. Take each rolled-out disk in your hands and place it on a baking pan. Using your fingers, gently start to press in the center to reach the bottom of the pan and then press the edges. Make sure the dough does not tear or warm up! Use your fingers to make the edges of the pies slightly wavy. Put them in the fridge while you make the pie filling. **B**

TO MAKE THE FILLING

1. Cut the strawberries into really tiny pieces.

2. In a small saucepan, combine the sugar, cornstarch, vanilla extract, and water until smooth. Add the chopped strawberries. Bring to the boil and stir until thickened, about 2 minutes. Remove from the heat. Refrigerate until slightly cooled.

3. Pour the cooked strawberry mixture in the pie crusts. Refrigerate until chilled and set. **C**

TO MAKE THE PIES

1. Roll out the other half of the dough. Cut out a circle of 2½ inches (6 cm) in diameter. These will be the tops of the pies.

2. Cut out circles of this top crust, all scattered, irregularly. The sizes of the circles are about 1 inch (2.5 cm) in diameter, ½ inch (1.25 cm), and ¼ inch (0.6 cm). Once this is done, lay this top part with the holes on top of the pie and press the edges to the side crust. Do the same with all 5 pies. **D**

3. Put them back in the fridge while you prepare the flowers.

4. Roll out the green dough real thin and cut out leaves. Set aside.

5. Roll out the red dough real thin and cut out flowers. Small and big ones, depending on the flower-shaped cookie cutters you have. Once they're done, set them aside too.

6. Take the 5 pies out of the fridge and use your own creativity to put the leaves and flowers on top. Use water or egg on the back of the flowers and leaves to get them to stick. (You can see my version of decoration in the photos.) **E**

7. Brush the tops of the dough with egg yolk.

8. Position an oven rack in the lower third of the oven, then place a baking sheet on the oven rack to catch any drips from the pies as they are baking.

9. Preheat the oven to 400°F (205°C, or gas mark 6).

10. Bake the pies on top of the hot baking sheet for 10 minutes, reduce the heat to 350°F (177°C, or gas mark 4), then continue to bake for 10 to 15 minutes, or until the crust is golden and the juices in the filling are bubbling.

11. If the crust begins to overbrown, cover the edges of the pies with aluminum foil and continue to bake until done. Let the pies cool for 1 hour before cutting to allow the filling to set.

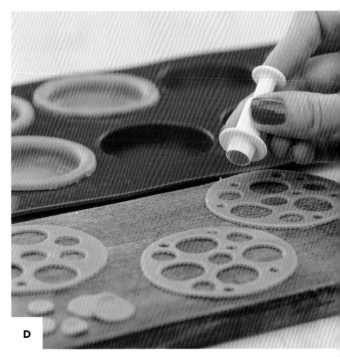

D

E

Pumpkin Pies

This is one of the best pumpkin pie recipes, but what takes it over the top is, of course, that pumpkin-shaped crust! Isn't it cute? Make a homemade pumpkin pie for Thanksgiving, or anytime you feel like eating one. (I like to make them at the first hint of fall.)

Tools & Materials

5 baking pans (2½ inches [6 cm] in diameter)

Rolling pin

Plastic wrap

Fondant embosser

YIELD: 5 PIES, ABOUT 2½ INCHES (6 CM) EACH

FOR CRUST

50 g store-bought dough or homemade dough (see the Apple Pies recipe, page 95)
Food coloring: green, brown, orange

FOR BRUSHING

19 g egg yolks (yolk from 1 large egg)

TIP If you use store-bought dough, you will need to roll it to about one-third the thickness (in other words, it comes in a thickness better suited to a "normal" pie than mini pies!).

FOR FILLING

30 g egg (about ⅔ large egg)
56 g pumpkin puree
31 g granulated sugar
1 teaspoon cornstarch
30 g heavy cream
8 g whole milk
¼ teaspoon cinnamon
¼ teaspoon ground ginger
¼ teaspoon ground nutmeg
¼ teaspoon ground cloves

TO PREPARE THE CRUSTS

1. Take about a peanut-size amount from the dough. Twice. Color 1 with green food coloring and the other with brown. Color the remaining dough with orange food coloring. This will make your pies. Roll out the dough. You will need about 100 g of dough per pie. Keep a small bowl of flour nearby to keep your work surface, rolling pin, and hands lightly floured. This prevents the pie dough from sticking. When rolling the pie dough out, always start from the center and work your way out in all directions, turning the dough as you go.

2. Smooth out the edges if you notice cracks. (If the pie dough feels too warm or the butter inside is melting, stop and chill the dough in the fridge for at least 10 minutes before continuing.)

3. From half of the dough, stretch 5 disks about 3½ inches (9 cm) in diameter for the 2½-inch (6-cm)-diameter baking pans. Take each rolled-out disk in your hands and place it on a baking pan. Using your fingers, gently start to press in the center to reach the bottom of the pan and then press the edges. Make sure the dough does not tear or warm up! Use your fingers to make the edges of the pies slightly wavy. Put them in the fridge while you make the pie filling. **A**

TO MAKE THE FILLING

1. Beat the egg in a small bowl. Whisk the pumpkin, sugar, cornstarch, heavy cream, milk, cinnamon, ginger, nutmeg, and cloves until completely combined, about 2 minutes. The mixture will be runny but will set up in the oven. Cover and refrigerate this filling.

2. Once cold, evenly spoon the filling into each unbaked crust, filling to the top. **B**

TO MAKE THE PIES

1. Roll out the other half of the dough and cut out five 2½-inch (6-cm)-diameter circles. Mark the center of the circles. Starting from here, make lines to the edge of the circles, as if you were cutting triangles, being careful not to cut the dough—just press a little deeper. This imitates the shape of a pumpkin. Draw about 8 of these "triangles" on the dough. **C**

2. Once done, place each crust on the pie and pinch the edges to prevent it from separating during baking. If you like, you can roll a small rim of the dough around the edge or braid a thin strip. Create freely!

3. In the middle of the pumpkin, form a small stem from the brown dough and some leaves from the green one. You can stick them on using water. **D**

4. Brush the top of the dough with the egg yolk.

5. Position an oven rack in the lower third of the oven, then place a baking sheet on the oven rack to catch any drips from the pies as they are baking.

6. Preheat the oven to 400°F (205°C, or gas mark 6).

7. Bake the pies on top of the hot baking sheet for 10 minutes, reduce the heat to 350°F (177°C, or gas mark 4), then continue to bake for 10 to 15 minutes, or until the crust is golden and juices in the filling are bubbling.

8. If the crust begins to overbrown, cover the edges of the pies with aluminum foil and continue to bake until done. Let the pies cool for 1 hour before cutting to allow the filling to set.

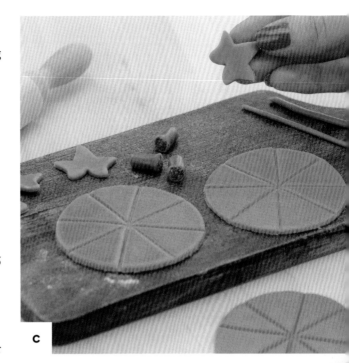

C

D

Peanut Butter & Marshmallow Pies

I love peanut butter, and what's more, I love it in (or on) just about anything baked. Of course, I love it spread on bread or layered inside a cake. And I can still remember the first day I made a peanut butter pie: Once I tasted it, I was hooked! I have eaten only few things more delicious than that pie. Are you curious? I'll show you how to make these mini versions—and with a little marshmallow on top for you fluffernutter fans.

Tools & Materials

Rolling pin

Five baking pans (2½ inches [6 cm] in diameter)

Plastic wrap

Parchment paper

Ceramic baking beans

YIELD: 5 PIES, ABOUT 2½ INCHES (6 CM) EACH

FOR CRUST

50 g store-bought dough or homemade dough (see the Apple Pies recipe, page 95)

FOR FILLING

28 g cream cheese, softened
12 g powdered sugar
32 g creamy peanut butter
30 g heavy cream
¼ teaspoon vanilla extract

FOR MARSHMALLOW

37 g granulated sugar
20 g water, divided
¼ teaspoon honey
2 g gelatin
Food coloring, if desired
Powdered sugar

FOR DECORATION

Sprinkles, chocolate chips, or powdered sugar, if desired

TIP If you use store-bought dough, you will need to roll it to about one-third the thickness (in other words, it comes in a thickness better suited to a "normal" pie than mini pies!).

TO PREPARE THE CRUSTS

1. Roll out the dough. Keep a small bowl of flour nearby to keep your work surface, rolling pin, and hands lightly floured. This prevents the pie dough from sticking. When rolling the pie dough out, always start from the center and work your way out in all directions, turning the dough as you go.

2. Smooth out the edges if you notice cracks. (If the pie dough feels too warm or the butter inside is melting, stop and chill the dough in the fridge for at least 10 minutes before continuing.)

3. From the dough, stretch 5 disks about 3½ inches (9 cm) in diameter for the 2½-inch (6-cm)-diameter baking pans. Take each rolled-out disk in your hands and place it on a baking pan. Using your fingers, gently start to press in the center to reach the

A

bottom of the pan and then press the edges. Make sure the dough does not tear or warm up! Use your fingers to make the edges of the pies slightly wavy. Put them in the fridge while you make the pie filling.

4. Position an oven rack in the lower third of the oven.

5. Preheat the oven to 400°F (205°C, or gas mark 6).

6. Put parchment paper or tin foil inside the pie crust and place ceramic baking beans on top. This way the pie crust will not puff up during baking. **A**

7. Bake the pie crust only (without the filling) for about 10 minutes, taking care not to overbrown it.

8. Cool completely on a wire rack while you prepare the filling and the marshmallow.

TO MAKE THE FILLING

1. In a small bowl, use an electric mixer to beat the cream cheese, powdered sugar, and peanut butter until light and fluffy, about 3 minutes.

2. In a separate bowl, use an electric mixer to whip the heavy cream until thick and light. Add the vanilla extract and continue to whip until stiff peaks form.

3. Gently fold the whipped cream into the peanut butter mixture. **B**

4. Pour into the prepared pie crust and freeze for 3 hours or chill in the fridge for at least 6 hours. **C**

B

TO MAKE THE MARSHMALLOW

1. Bring the sugar to a boil with 15 g of water and the honey in a small saucepan, then simmer over a low heat for 3 to 4 minutes.

2. Meanwhile, dissolve the gelatin powder in the remaining 5 g of water.

3. Add some of the hot syrup to the gelatin and whisk to combine, then add the rest of the syrup.

4. Start whisking on low speed for about 3 to 4 minutes.

5. Then stir on high heat for 1 to 2 minutes. The resulting mass, if not colored, should whiten and become a sticky, gooey consistency.

6. If you want to color with food coloring, add it now. You can also separate the mass into several portions and color it with different colors. In a few strokes, stir the colored mixture to form a layer of marshmallows with a transition of colors. **D**

7. Pour the prepared syrup onto parchment paper dusted with powdered sugar. Leave to stand in the fridge for 1 to 2 hours, then cut into small cubes and pile on top of the pies. You can add sprinkles or chocolate chips, or just a little powdered sugar.

Note You can also use store-bought mini marshmallows (that's what I did) or marshmallow cream and spread it on top instead of making homemade marshmallow.

C

D

Lemon Meringue Pies

These are the best lemon meringue pies! The tart yet creamy lemon custard filling is topped with mile-high billowy meringue. (Okay, at tiny size, maybe more like an inch high?!) Make these pies when you want an impressive dessert. If you have a tiny knife, this is a superfun pie to cut slices as the layers hold up well.

FOR CRUST

50 g store-bought dough or homemade dough (see the Apple Pies recipe, page 95)

FOR FILLING

19 g egg yolk (yolk from 1 large egg)
64 g water
40 g granulated sugar
7.5 g cornstarch
Pinch of salt
23 g lemon juice
5.5 g unsalted butter, softened

FOR MERINGUE

30 g egg whites (white from 1 large egg)
20 g granulated sugar
Food coloring, if desired

Tools & Materials

Rolling pin
5 baking pans (2½ inch [6 cm] in diameter)
Plastic wrap
Parchment paper
Ceramic baking beans
Electric mixer
Piping bag
Round decorating nozzle (about ¼ inch [0.6 cm] in diameter)

YIELD: 5 PIES, ABOUT 2½ INCHES (6 CM) EACH

TIP If you use store-bought dough, you will need to roll it to about one-third the thickness (in other words, it comes in a thickness better suited to a "normal" pie than mini pies!).

TO PREPARE THE CRUSTS

1. Roll out the dough. Keep a small bowl of flour nearby to keep your work surface, rolling pin, and hands lightly floured. This prevents the pie dough from sticking. When rolling the pie dough out, always start from the center and work your way out in all directions, turning the dough as you go.

2. Smooth out the edges if you notice cracks. (If the pie dough feels too warm or the butter inside is melting, stop and chill the dough in the fridge for at least 10 minutes before continuing.)

3. From half of the dough, stretch 5 disks about 3½ inches (9 cm) in diameter for the 2½-inch (6-cm)-diameter baking pans. Take each rolled-out disk in your hands and place it on a baking pan. Using your fingers, gently start to press in the center to reach the bottom of the pan and then press the edges. Make sure the dough does not tear or warm up! Use your fingers to make the edges of the pies slightly wavy. Put them in the fridge while you make the pie filling.

4. Position an oven rack in the lower third of the oven.

5. Preheat the oven to 400°F (205°C, or gas mark 6).

6. Put parchment paper or tin foil inside the pie and place ceramic baking beans on top. This way the pie crust will not puff up during baking. Bake only the pie crust (without the filling) for about 10 minutes, taking care not to overbrown it. **A**

7. Cool completely on a wire rack while you prepare the filling and the meringue.

TO MAKE THE FILLING

1. Whisk the egg yolk in a small bowl or liquid measuring cup. Set aside. Whisk the water, granulated sugar, cornstarch, salt, and lemon juice together in a small saucepan over medium heat. The mixture will be thin and cloudy, then eventually begin thickening and bubbling after about 3 minutes. Once thickened, give it a whisk and reduce heat to low.

2. Very slowly stream a few large spoonfuls of warm lemon mixture into the beaten egg yolk. Then, also in a very slow stream, pour the egg yolk mixture back into the saucepan while whisking. Turn heat back up to medium. Cook until the mixture is thick and big bubbles begin bursting at the surface.

3. Remove the pan from the heat and whisk in the butter. Spread the filling into the partially baked crusts. **B**

4. Set the pies aside while you make the meringue. Do not cool completely; it should stay a little warm.

TO MAKE THE MERINGUE

1. With a handheld electric mixer or a stand mixer fitted with a whisk attachment, beat the egg white on low speed for 1 minute, then increase to high speed until soft peaks form, about 4 more minutes.

2. Put the egg white in a small bowl. Whisk to soft peaks, then add the powdered sugar, a spoonful at a time, whisking between each addition without overbeating.

3. If you like, you can color the meringue with a little food coloring (you can even make a multicolored one).

TO MAKE THE PIES

1. Fill the meringue into a piping bag with a round decorating nozzle. Press small swirls on top of the pie, working from the outside inward to prevent the meringue from sinking. **C**

2. Return to the oven for 5 to 7 minutes until the meringue is crisp and slightly colored. Let the pies sit in the pan for 30 minutes, then remove and leave for at least another 30 minutes before slicing.

Blueberry Pies

Blueberry pie is a classic, and these pies deliver on that timeless blueberry filling flavor. But the real showstopper here is the decoration. Unlike most of the pies in this chapter, we are going the extra mile with this one and making them owl-shaped so that everyone will be asking "whoooo, whoooo made these?!" When serving, place a few (clean) twigs on the plate so that your owl pies can "sit" on a tree branch. Everyone will love these bite-size pies!

FOR CRUST
28 g stick unsalted butter
70 g all-purpose flour
¼ teaspoon salt
½ teaspoon sugar
28 g sour cream (full-fat)

FOR BRUSHING
19 g egg yolks (yolk from
   1 large egg)

FOR DECORATION
Powdered sugar

FOR FILLING
9 g granulated sugar
1 g cornstarch
1 g allspice
1 g cinnamon
Pinch of lemon zest
60 g blueberries

Tools & Materials

Plastic wrap

Rolling pin

5 baking pans (2½ inches
   [6 cm] in diameter)

Pen

Paper

Scissors

**YIELD: 5 PIES, ABOUT
2½ INCHES (6 CM) EACH**

TIP If you use store-bought dough, you will need to roll it to about one-third the thickness (in other words, it comes in a thickness better suited to a "normal" pie than mini pies!).

TO MAKE THE DOUGH

1. Cut the butter into cubes and let them sit on a plate so that the butter is not freezing cold, but it shouldn't warm up!

2. In a small bowl, vigorously whisk the flour, salt, and sugar.

3. Places the cubes of butter in the flour mixture. Use clean hands to squish the flour and butter together with your fingers, then your knuckles. **A**

4. Add the sour cream and use a fork to incorporate it into the mixture. You now have pie dough!

A

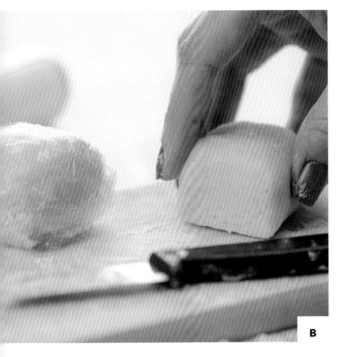

B

5. Place the pie dough on a lightly floured work surface (for example, a table). Using floured hands, fold the dough into itself until the flour is fully incorporated. Form it into a ball. Don't worry about overworking this dough. Just form it in a way that there are no cracks on it.

6. Divide the dough into 2 halves and flatten into 2 disks. Sprinkle them all over with a little flour. Wrap tightly with plastic wrap and refrigerate for at least 2 hours. **B**

7. After the dough has chilled, it's time to roll it out. Keep a small bowl of flour nearby to keep your work surface, rolling pin, and hands lightly floured. This prevents the pie dough from sticking. When rolling the pie dough out, always start from the center and work your way out in all directions, turning the dough as you go.

8. Smooth out the edges if you notice cracks. (If the pie dough feels too warm or the butter inside is melting, stop and chill the dough in the fridge for at least 10 minutes before continuing.)

9. From half of the dough, stretch 5 disks about 3½ inches (9 cm) in diameter for the 2½-inch (6-cm)-diameter baking pans. Take each rolled-out disk in your hands and place it on a baking pan. Using your fingers, gently start to press in the center to reach the bottom of the pan and then press the edges. Make sure the dough does not tear or warm up! Use your fingers to make the edges of the pies slightly wavy. Put them in the fridge while you make the pie filling. **C**

C

TO MAKE THE FILLING

1. In a small bowl, stir together the sugar, cornstarch, lemon peel, allspice, cinnamon, and salt.

2. Add the blueberries and gently toss to combine.

3. Pour the blueberry filling into the prepared pie crusts, then place in the fridge while you prepare the patterned crusts.

TO MAKE THE PIES

1. Roll out the other half of the dough, as thin as the previous batch. Draw the pattern in the dough with a toothpick to make your owl (see photos). Using a small knife, cut the patterns out of the dough and place them on top of the filling. **D, E**

2. Brush the top of the dough with egg yolk.

3. Position an oven rack in the lower third of the oven, then place a baking sheet on the oven rack to catch any drips from the pies as they are baking.

4. Preheat the oven to 400°F (205°C, or gas mark 6).

5. Bake the pies on top of the hot baking sheet for 20 minutes, reduce the heat to 350°F (177°C, or gas mark 4), then continue to bake for 35 to 45 minutes, or until the crust is golden and juices in the filling are bubbling.

6. If the crust begins to overbrown, cover the edges of the pies with aluminum foil and continue to bake until done.

7. Let the pies cool for 2 to 3 hours before cutting to allow the filling to set. Sprinkle with powdered sugar. **F**

D

E

F

6

Brownies, Bars & Other Sweet Treats

Peanut Butter Crispy Rice Brownies

Why choose between crispy treats and brownies when you can have both? These easy peanut butter crispy rice brownies combine two favorites into one tasty dessert. These things are dangerously delicious!

Tools & Materials

Small baking pan (about 4 x 9 inches [10 x 23 cm])

Parchment paper

Small saucepan and a heat-proof metal bowl (see Tip on page 40)

Electric mixer

YIELD: 25 BROWNIES

FOR BROWNIES

31 g unsalted butter, softened
31 g chocolate
45 g eggs (about 1 large egg)
84 g granulated sugar
29 g all-purpose flour
7.5 g cocoa powder
¼ teaspoon vanilla extract
Pinch of salt

FOR PEANUT BUTTER FILLING

130 g chunky peanut butter
50 g powdered sugar

FOR CEREAL FILLING

70 g peanut butter
85 g white chocolate chips
22 g colorful crisped rice cereal

TO MAKE THE BROWNIES

1. Preheat the oven to 350°F (177°C, or gas mark 4) or 320°F (160°C, or gas mark 3) fan forced. Grease the baking pan or line it with parchment paper.

2. Take a small saucepan and heat-proof metal bowl that matches in size. Bring the water in the saucepan to a boil.

3. Place the butter and chocolate in the heat-proof bowl over the saucepan of simmering water (don't let the bowl touch the water). Stir with a metal spoon until the chocolate is melted, then remove from the heat.

4. With a whisk, quickly stir in the egg, sugar, flour, cocoa powder, vanilla extract, and salt until just combined. Pour the mixture into the prepared baking pan. Bake for 30 minutes or until a toothpick inserted in the center comes out with moist crumbs on it. Set aside to cool completely.

5. Don't take it out of the pan!

TO MAKE THE TOPPING

1. For the peanut butter topping, whisk chunky peanut butter and powdered sugar, then spread it over the cooled brownies. **A**

2. For the crisped rice filling, put smooth peanut butter and chocolate chips in a small bowl. Pop it in the microwave on 50% power for 10-second increments until melted, then stir until smooth. Mix in the crisped rice cereal until well coated.

3. Spoon it over the brownies and spread evenly, pressing down gently. The colorful pieces will stand out beautifully! **B, C**

4. Refrigerate for 1 hour before slicing.

5. If you like, you can put some melted chocolate on top!

A

B

C

Small baking pan (about 4 x 9 inches [10 x 23 cm])

Parchment paper

Small saucepan and a heat-proof metal bowl (see Tip on page 40)

Paper

Pen

Scissors

Sieve

YIELD: 25 BROWNIES

Classic Brownies

A brownie is a dessert that is extremely easy to make, and almost impossible to stop eating! No matter how much you make, they seem to be gone in no time. In this recipe, I'm sharing one of my favorite brownie recipes as well as a quick and easy decoration technique to personalize them.

31 g unsalted butter, softened
31 g milk chocolate
45 g eggs (about 1 large egg)
84 g granulated sugar
29 g all-purpose flour

7.5 g cocoa powder
¼ teaspoon vanilla extract
Pinch of salt
50 g powdered sugar

TO MAKE THE BROWNIES

1. Preheat the oven to 350°F (177°C, or gas mark 4) or 320°F (160°C, or gas mark 3) fan forced. Grease the baking pan or line it with parchment paper.

2. Take a small saucepan and heat-proof metal bowl that matches in size. Bring the water in the saucepan to a boil.

3. Place the butter and chocolate in the heat-proof bowl over the saucepan of simmering water (don't let the bowl touch the water). Stir with a metal spoon until the chocolate is melted, then remove from the heat.

4. With a whisk, quickly stir in the egg, sugar, flour, cocoa powder, vanilla extract, and salt until just combined. Pour the mixture into the prepared baking pan. Bake for 30 minutes or until a toothpick inserted in the center comes out with moist crumbs on it. Set aside to cool completely.

5. Remove the cooled brownie from the baking pan. Cut the brownie into 1 x 1-inch (2.5 x-2.5-cm) pieces.

A

B

FOR DECORATION

1. Take a sheet of paper. Cut it into 1 x 1-inch (2.5 x 2.5-cm) pieces. Then draw a pattern of your choice on the paper and cut it out. For example, I drew a heart shape and the name of the person I surprised with my brownies. **A**

2. After cutting out the shape you want, place it onto a piece of brownie, then put powdered sugar in a sieve and sift onto the white sheet. The brownie will only have powdered sugar where the cut-out pattern is! **B**

Be creative!

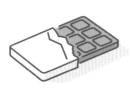

Salted Caramel Bars

How does a layer of rich, buttery, salted caramel topping on a light, flaky, and delicious shortbread sound? These bite-size treats pack a ton of decadent flavor.

Tools & Materials

Electric mixer

Small baking pan (about 4 inches [10 cm] in diameter)

Sugar thermometer

YIELD: 6 BARS

FOR SHORTBREAD
28 g unsalted butter, softened
12 g powdered sugar
Pinch of salt
¼ teaspoon vanilla extract
Food coloring: green
35 g all-purpose flour

FOR CARAMEL
30 g unsalted butter
80 g granulated sugar
20 g brown sugar
Pinch of salt
68 g heavy cream

FOR DECORATION
10 g fondant icing paste
Food coloring: brown, black

TO MAKE THE SHORTBREAD

1. Put the butter into a large bowl and beat well with a wooden spoon or an electric mixer until creamy and pale. Add the sugar, salt, and vanilla and beat again until even paler. Add a small amount of green food coloring to get a pale green color.

2. Add the flour to the butter mixture. Using a spatula, gently work the flour into the mixture to make a dough that starts to clump together.

3. Press the dough into the baking pan, then level and smooth it with the back of a spoon. Prick it all over with a fork, then let it chill for 10 minutes, or longer if you like, until firm. Meanwhile, preheat the oven to 325°F (163°C, or gas mark 3). **A**

4. Bake for 25 to 30 minutes, or until the shortbread is golden all over. Let cool completely.

A

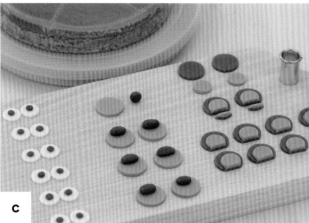

B

C

TO MAKE THE CARAMEL

1. Mix the butter, granulated sugar, brown sugar, salt, and heavy cream in a medium-size, heavy-bottomed saucepan. The caramel will bubble up as it cooks.

2. Bring the mixture to a boil, stirring occasionally, and make sure that all the sugar is dissolved. Once it's boiling, insert a sugar thermometer and cook until it reads 250°F (120°C, or gas mark 1/2), stirring occasionally.

3. Once at the right temperature, remove the pan from the heat, stir in the vanilla extract, then mix for 6 to 8 minutes with an electric mixer to get the frothier consistency you need. Then pour the caramel on top of the shortbread. **B**

4. Let the caramel sit until firm, about 2 to 3 hours at room temperature.

5. Once set, remove from the mold and cut into smaller bars.

6. Now it's time for decorating. Make teddy bear faces on each bar. For that, you need ears, a nose, a mouth, and eyes.

7. Get the fondant icing paste. Divide it into 2 halves. Color one-half light brown, and divide the other half into 3 portions. Color 2 of them dark brown and black while leaving the last portion white.

8. Make the ears, nose, and eyes, then place these on the bars. **C, D**

Remember, you can decorate with any animal of your choice!

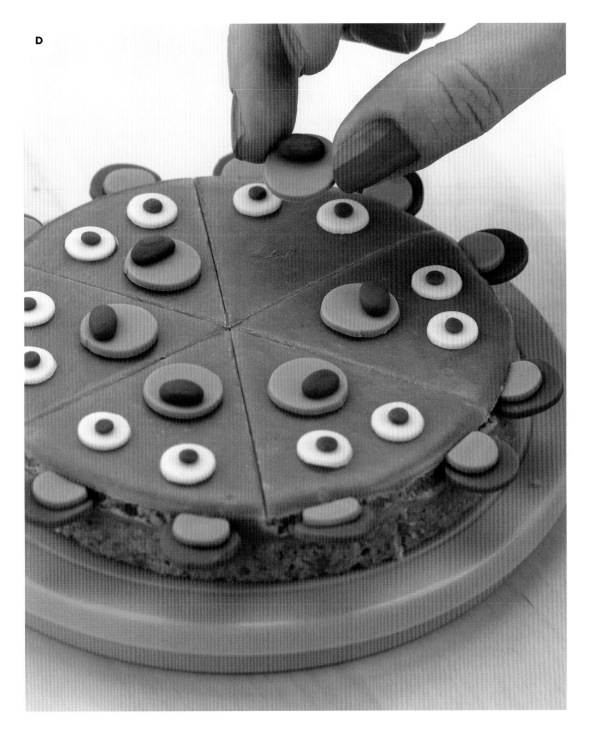

D

Chocolate-Hazelnut Puff Pastry Treats

Puff pastry is notoriously time-consuming and difficult to make at home. Thank goodness the premade versions you can find in the refridgerator section of the supermarket have come a long way in the past few years! This recipe is all about taking the easy-to-work-with premade puff and forming it into something fun—be it snails, bars, or trees! The tree shapes in particular are perfect for Christmas. I strongly recommend you try the chocolate-hazelnut filling, but of course the only limit on fillings is your imagination. Also try these with jam or even a savory filling or spread.

FOR PUFF PASTRY TREATS
1 packet puff pastry
   (store-bought)
20 g chocolate-hazelnut spread

FOR BRUSHING
19 g egg yolks (yolk from
   1 large egg)
¼ teaspoon whole milk

FOR DECORATION
Powdered sugar
Sprinkles
Red gummy candies
White chocolate callets
Food coloring

TO PREPARE THE PUFF PASTRY

1. Preheat the oven to 350°F (177°C, or gas mark 4). Grease the baking pan or line it with parchment paper.

2. Cut a whole sheet of puff pastry into rectangles of 4 x 3 inches (10 x 8 cm).

Tools & Materials
Small baking pan
(9 x 5 inches [24 x 13 cm])

Parchment paper

Small saucepan and
   heat-proof metal bowl
   (see Tip on page 40)

Sieve

**YIELD: 3 TREES, 20 SNAILS,
10 BARS**

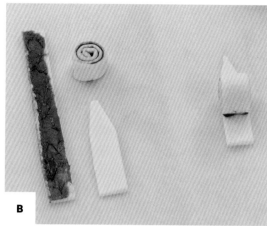

A **B**

TO MAKE THE TREE PUFF PASTRY

1. Cut out your pastry into a pine tree shape. Lay two frozen puff pastry rectangles on top of each other and cut through them to get 2 of the same tree. Don't have them sit on top of each other for too long though, or they will soften and it will be extremely difficult to peel them apart!

2. Place the cut-out pine tree shape on parchment paper. Be careful not to cut the paper later.

3. Take the top pastry off. Spread the chocolate-hazelnut spread on the bottom one. **A**

4. Place the removed pastry next to it and cut out the branches on both sides all the way to the top. Peel them apart and spread the chocolate-hazelnut spread on the bottom one again.

5. After spreading each with the chocolate-hazelnut spread, twist each branch so that they resemble twisted breadsticks. By this stage, your pastry will have started to soften, making cutting so much easier. Just be patient and careful not to tear the pastry when lifting the knife after each cut.

6. Brush the pastry with egg yolk mixed with milk and put in the oven for 10 to 15 minutes.

7. After cooling, sprinkle with a little powdered sugar or Christmas sprinkles.

Voilà, beautiful puff pastry
Christmas tree treats!

TO MAKE THE SNAIL PUFF PASTRY

1. Spread the puff pastry sheet. Cut ½-inch (1.25-cm)-thick strips from it.

2. You'll need a 1-inch (2.5-cm)-long strip for one snail. This will make the body of the snail. And you'll also need a 4-inch (10-cm)-long strip. Spread this strip with the chocolate-hazelnut spread and roll it up. This will be the shell of the snail. **B**

3. Put a small blob of the chocolate-hazelnut spread in the middle of the shorter piece and sit the pastry shell on top, making sure they are securely attached.

C

4. Repeat the process with all the snails, then brush each with the eggy mixture and place them on a baking sheet and bake for 12 to 15 minutes, until the pastry is risen and golden.

5. After cooling, you can imitate the tentacles of the snail with red gummy candies.

TO MAKE THE COOKIE BAR PUFF PASTRY

1. Lay the puff pastry sheet flat. Spread the chocolate-hazelnut spread on 1 strip and lay another strip on it.

2. Cut strips ½-inch (1.25-cm) thick and about 2 inches (5 cm) long. Holding by the ends, twist the pastry. Be careful not to tear it. **C**

3. Place the twisted bars on parchment paper side by side, brush them with the eggy mixture, and bake for about 10 minutes, until golden brown.

4. Remove from the oven and let cool.

5. Melt the white chocolate callets as you learned in the cake pops recipes (pages 27–42). Color the chocolate as you desire.

6. Dip about one-third of the bars in the melted chocolate and decorate with the rainbow sprinkles.

7. Place them in a glass and serve!

Brownie Lollipops

These chocolate chip "lollipops" combine two classic desserts into one epic sweet treat. With crunchy chocolate icing and colorful candies on top, they are eye-catching as well. If you have leftover brownies at the end, use them to make colorful cake pops (see pages 27-42)!

Tools & Materials

Electric mixer

Small baking pan (about 4 x 9 inches [10 x 23 cm])

Parchment paper

Small saucepan and heat-proof metal bowl (see Tip on page 40)

Ice cream sticks

YIELD: 15 LOLLIPOPS

FOR COOKIES

28 g unsalted butter, softened
40 g brown sugar
13 g granulated sugar
30 g eggs (about ⅔ large egg)
¼ teaspoon vanilla extract
52 g all-purpose flour
¼ teaspoon baking soda
42 g milk chocolate chips

FOR BROWNIES

31 g unsalted butter, softened
31 g milk chocolate

45 g eggs (about 1 large egg)
84 g granulated sugar
29 g all-purpose flour
7.5 g cocoa powder
¼ teaspoon vanilla extract
Pinch of salt

FOR DECORATION

50 g white chocolate callets
Food coloring: blue, orange
Sprinkles

TO MAKE THE COOKIES

1. Using an electric mixer, combine the butter with the brown sugar and granulated sugar in a small bowl. Add the egg, mixing for 30 to 60 seconds. Batter will thicken and lighten in color. Stir in the vanilla extract.

2. Stir in the flour and baking soda. It will take a minute for the dough to come together as you stir it, but it will! Stir in the chocolate chips.

TO MAKE THE BROWNIES

1. Preheat the oven to 350°F (177°C, or gas mark 4) or 320°F (160°C, or gas mark 3) fan forced. Grease the baking pan or line it with parchment paper.

2. Take a small saucepan and heat-proof metal bowl that matches in size. Bring the water in the saucepan to a boil.

3. Place the butter and chocolate in the heat-proof bowl over the saucepan of simmering water (don't let the bowl touch the water). Stir with a metal spoon until the chocolate is melted, then remove from the heat.

4. With a whisk, quickly stir in the egg, sugar, flour, cocoa powder, vanilla extract, and salt until just combined. Pour the mixture into the prepared cake pan.

5. Scoop roughly rounded tablespoons of cookie dough and press slightly into the brownie batter. Add more chocolate chips to the top of the cookie dough and brownies, if you like. **A**

6. Bake for 30 minutes or until a toothpick inserted in the center comes out with moist crumbs on it. Set aside to cool completely.

7. Remove the cooled brownie from the baking pan. Cut into rectangles: ½ x 1½ inches (1.25 x 3.75 cm).

TO MAKE THE BROWNIE POPS

1. Now it's time to use the saucepan and the metal bowl again (though make sure they are cleaned well before using them!). Melt a small amount of the white chocolate callets over the boiling water, stirring constantly. Dip the tip of an ice cream stick into the white chocolate and then insert into a brownie rectangle. **B**

2. Once you have finished all the rectangles, divide the remaining chocolate into 3 portions and color them. Once the desired color is achieved, pour the 3 colors together and mix a few times with a spoon to create a swirl of colors (or use them separately). **C**

3. One by one, dip the brownie rectangles into the chocolate. You can dip them all the way in, or only halfway or just 1 corner. Once the excess chocolate has dripped off, add sprinkles to the brownies, and they are ready! **D**

Homemade Sandwich Cookies

Oh sure, it is easy to buy similar cookies at the store, but these are easy enough to make and filled with none of the mysterious ingredients needed to keep them shelf-stable for months! (Also, good luck finding sandwich cookies at the store that are this tiny.) Packed with chocolate flavor and a complementary creamy filling, there is one important similarity to the store-bought version: It's impossible to eat just one.

Tools & Materials

Electric mixer

Small baking sheet

Parchment paper or silicone baking mat

Rolling pin

Piping bags

YIELD: 20 SANDWICH COOKIES

FOR COOKIES

50 g all-purpose flour
¼ teaspoon baking soda
Pinch of salt
29 g unsalted butter, softened
50 g granulated sugar
20 g eggs (about ⅓ large egg)
¼ teaspoon vanilla extract
Food coloring: orange

FOR FILLING

20 g unsalted butter, softened
52 g powdered sugar
¼ teaspoon vanilla extract
Food coloring: green (additional colors if desired)

FOR DECORATION

Food coloring pen
Melted white chocolate
Food coloring

TO PREPARE THE COOKIES

1. Put the flour, baking soda, and salt together in a small bowl. Set aside.

2. Using an electric mixer, beat the butter on high speed until creamy, for about 1 minute. Scrape down the sides and the bottom of the bowl as needed. Switch the mixer to medium speed and beat in the granulated sugar. Beat in the egg, vanilla extract, and orange food coloring. Turn the mixer off and pour the dry ingredients into the wet ingredients. Turn the mixer on low and slowly beat until a dough is formed. Cover the dough tightly with plastic wrap and chill for 30 minutes.

3. Preheat the oven to 350°F (177°C, or gas mark 4). Remove the cookie dough from the refrigerator. Line the baking sheet with parchment paper or a silicone baking mat. Set aside.

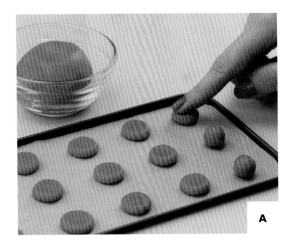

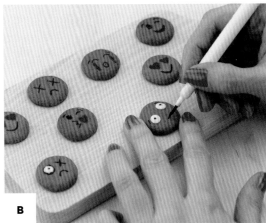

A

B

4. Roll the dough into small balls, about ½ inch (1.25 cm). Slightly flatten the balls. Bake each batch for 6 to 8 minutes. These cookies bake very quickly because they are small. They will appear soft when done. Remove from the oven and allow to cool for at least 5 minutes on the baking sheet before transferring to a wire rack to cool completely. **A**

TO MAKE THE FILLING

1. With an electric mixer, beat the butter on medium speed until creamy, about 1 minute. Add the powdered sugar and vanilla extract. Beat on low speed for 30 seconds, then increase to medium-high speed and beat for 1 full minute. Taste.

2. Divide the frosting into as many portions as the number of colors you want. Add the food colorings and stir well. Repeat these steps until you get the desired color. I only made green this time.

3. Pour it into the piping bag, then, using scissors, cut a medium-size hole at the tip of the piping bag. Set aside.

TO ASSEMBLE THE SANDWICH COOKIES

1. Before filling your little sandwich cookies, draw faces on them. All kinds of faces! Crying, laughing, smiling, angry . . . **B**

2. You can also do this with a food coloring pen, or you can melt white chocolate, color it the color you want, fill it into a piping bag, and after cutting a small hole at the tip, you can draw on the cookies. (See the method for melting chocolate in one of the cake pops recipes, pages 27-42.)

3. Once the chocolate has set, turn the cookies upside down. Pair them together (one-half with a face design and the other half blank). Get the piping bag and pipe the filling on the empty half, then put the top layer onto it. Repeat this step with all the cookies.

What an impressive little crew you have created!

Acknowledgments

I would like to gratefully thank all those who believed in me and without whom this little book would not have been possible.

Many thanks to my editor, Thom, for always being patient with the many questions I had. Thanks for all the ideas and positive feedback, which let me know that I was on the right track. I am very grateful for all the help and this book is complete because of him.

I also want to thank my editorial project manager, Gabrielle, for always giving me detailed answers to my questions; it was a pleasure to work with her.

One of the biggest thanks goes to my photographer, Janos Vass, who kept me going on many occasions when something didn't turn out as I had planned. His words and support gave me the strength to carry on, and his enthusiasm always flowed through to me. I loved watching his photo shoots, which were often coupled with almost acrobatic elements. He has put his heart and soul into these photos, just as I put my heart and soul into my cookies. Without him, this book would not have been accomplished.

The ultimate "thank you" goes to my mother. She has always believed in me, no matter how impossible my plans seemed. She helped me in every way she could. She was my chief taster and my greatest support. While writing this book, I reminisced about the memories of being a little girl and baking cookies with my mom. Every time, I would make a miniature version of her cake. That's where this love of mine for mini baking and cooking stemmed from and it made the book possible! Thank you for everything!!!!

Finally, thank YOU, my dear reader! I wish you the same joy in making tiny dishes as I have had in making this book for you. Don't be discouraged if you don't succeed at first... Remember that even I didn't succeed at first. I hope you'll put this book aside one day with memories you'll look back on with pleasure as an adult! And maybe one day . . . you will bake from it again . . . but with your child!

About the Author

Jennifer Ziemons is the creator behind *Jenny's Mini Cooking Show*. She is a former professional baker, winner of the IKA Culinary Olympics gold medal as a sugar and cake artist, and a four-time gold medal winner at the Cake International competition in England. Jenny has since grown a substantial audience on YouTube and has been featured on a variety of sites thanks to her unique expertise in miniature baking. Her work has also been featured in sets and commercials for major brands, such as Haribo and Schwarzkopf.

Index